For the place that shaped me
and
for Sam, *"without whom ... "*

ACKNOWLEDGMENTS

In the development of this play from its original idea through several drafts and two staged productions there are many people who made significant and invaluable contributions — foremost among them are the incomparable Julie Harris and the two exceptional companies. And, most especially, Gordon Edelstein. To all of them my thanks and admiration.

SCENT OF THE ROSES
Copyright © 2001, Lisette Lecat Ross

All Rights Reserved

CAUTION: Professionals and amateurs are hereby warned that performance of SCENT OF THE ROSES is subject to payment of a royalty. It is fully protected under the copyright laws of the United States of America, and of all countries covered by the International Copyright Union (including the Dominion of Canada and the rest of the British Commonwealth), and of all countries covered by the Pan-American Copyright Convention, the Universal Copyright Convention, the Berne Convention, and of all countries with which the United States has reciprocal copyright relations. All rights, including professional/amateur stage rights, motion picture, recitation, lecturing, public reading, radio broadcasting, television, video or sound recording, all other forms of mechanical or electronic reproduction, such as CD-ROM, CD-I, DVD, information storage and retrieval systems and photocopying, and the rights of translation into foreign languages, are strictly reserved. Particular emphasis is placed upon the matter of readings, permission for which must be secured from the Author's agent in writing.

The English language stock and amateur stage performance rights in the United States, its territories, possessions and Canada for SCENT OF THE ROSES are controlled exclusively by DRAMATISTS PLAY SERVICE, INC., 440 Park Avenue South, New York, NY 10016. No professional or non-professional performance of the Play may be given without obtaining in advance the written permission of DRAMATISTS PLAY SERVICE, INC., and paying the requisite fee.

Inquiries concerning all other rights should be addressed to William Morris Agency, Inc., 1325 Avenue of the Americas, 15th Floor, New York, NY 10019. Attn: Samuel Liff.

SPECIAL NOTE
Anyone receiving permission to produce SCENT OF THE ROSES is required to give credit to the Author as sole and exclusive Author of the Play on the title page of all programs distributed in connection with performances of the Play and in all instances in which the title of the Play appears for purposes of advertising, publicizing or otherwise exploiting the Play and/or a production thereof. The name of the Author must appear on a separate line, in which no other name appears, immediately beneath the title and in size of type equal to 50% of the size of the largest, most prominent letter used for the title of the Play. No person, firm or entity may receive credit larger or more prominent than that accorded the Author. The following acknowledgment must appear on the title page in all programs distributed in connection with performances of the Play:

"Scent of the Roses" was originally produced by
A Contemporary Theatre, Seattle, Washington
Gordon Edelstein, Artistic Director

Subsequently produced by the Helen Hayes
Performing Arts Center, Nyack, New York
Tony Stimac, Executive Producer; Rod Kaats, Artistic Director

SCENT OF THE ROSES received its world premiere at A Contemporary Theatre (Gordon Edelstein, Artistic Director; Susan B. Trapnell, Managing Director) in Seattle, Washington, on July 17, 1998. It was directed by Gordon Edelstein; the assistant director was Valerie Curtis-Newton; the set design was by Thomas Lynch; the lighting design was by Peter Kaczorowski; the composer and sound designer was John Gromada; the costume design was by Martin Pakledinaz; the dialect coach was David Morden; the artist was Steven La Rose; the dramaturg was Liz Engelman; and the stage manager was Jeffrey K. Hanson. The cast was as follows:

ANNALISE MORANT	Julie Harris
IMOGEN	Jeanne Paulsen
NIGEL	Jay Patterson
KATE	Kate Forbes
YOUNG ANNALISE	Jessalyn Gilsig
MARAAI	Kirsten Williamson
JULIUS VAN GEORGE	Ntare Mwine
ALISTAIR LEYTON-CLARKE	William Biff McGuire
TSHIPI	Bobby Bermea
SERENA	Sheila Williams

SCENT OF THE ROSES was subsequently produced at the Helen Hayes Performing Arts Center (Rod Kaats, Artistic Director; Tony Stimac, Executive Producer; Marilyn Stimac, Associate Producer) in Nyack, New York, on October 30, 1999. It was directed by Gordon Edelstein; the set design was by Thomas Lynch; the associate set designer was Curtis Wallin; the lighting design was by Renée Molina; the composer and sound designer was John Gromada; the costume design was by Martin Pakledinaz; the production stage manager was Mitchell Erickson; and the stage manager was John Handy. The cast was as follows:

ANNALISE MORANT	Julie Harris
IMOGEN	Jeanne Paulsen
NIGEL	Jay Patterson
KATE	Kate Forbes
YOUNG ANNALISE	Jessalyn Gilsig
MARAAI	Myra Lucretia Taylor
JULIUS VAN GEORGE	Peter Francis James
ALISTAIR LEYTON-CLARKE	Remak Ramsay
TSHIPI	Akili Prince
SERENA	Laurine Towler

CHARACTERS

ANNALISE MORANT, a white woman in her late sixties.

YOUNG ANNALISE (née Wynand)

NIGEL MORANT, Annalise's son, early forties.

IMOGEN ELLIS, Annalise's older daughter, mid to late forties.

KATE MORANT, Annalise's younger daughter, late thirties.

JULIUS VAN GEORGE, a light-skinned Coloured man, in his early to mid thirties; a painter.

MARAAI MATTHYS, a coloured woman of indeterminate age, early to late thirties.

ALISTAIR LEYTON-CLARKE, an urbane Englishman anywhere from his late fifties into his seventies, an art dealer.

TSHIPI SIBEKO, an African in his early twenties.

SERENA CLAASENS, a light-skinned Coloured woman in her late forties/early fifties.

PLACE

South Africa

TIME

The Present

ACT ONE

Scene 1: Annalise's living room.
Scene 2: Flashback to 1951. Slade River.
Scene 3: An office in Johannesburg. Some days later.
Scene 4: Annalise's living room. Later that evening.
Scene 5: Flashback to early 1952. Slade River.
Scene 6: Annalise's living room. An hour or so later.
Scene 7: An office in Johannesburg. Some days later.
Scene 8: Annalise's living room. Later that same night.

ACT TWO

Scene 1: Annalise's living room. A day later.
Scene 2: Flashback to early 1960. Slade River.
Scene 3: Annalise's living room. A few days later.
Scene 4: The same. Some days later.
Scene 5: The same. Some days later.
Scene 6: The poor section of Slade River. The next day.
Scene 7: The rose park. Two days later.
　Flashback to late 1951. Slade River.
Scene 8: The rose park, an hour or so later.
Scene 9: An office in Johannesburg. Four months later.
　Flashback to 1951. Slade River.

NOTE ON THE LANGUAGE

A guide to the pronunciation of Afrikaans and Sesotho is given in the International Phonetic Alphabet in appendices at the back of the text. An idiomatic English translation of the words/phrases follows immediately in the text in *["italics with quotation marks, between square brackets"]*.

NOTE ON THE CHARACTERS

With most South African plays, given that country's historical and socio-political reality, it is necessary to stipulate the race of the characters. The word "Coloured," in official use in that country, designates any person of "mixed blood."

SCENT OF THE ROSES

ACT ONE

Scene 1

Annalise Morant's living room. A midweek night, after dinner.

The furnishings are modest. The only really remarkable item in the room is a painting — a vibrant landscape of an undulating mountain with open African countryside in the foreground.

The lights come up on Annalise (a white woman in her late sixties, early seventies) and her children, Imogen Ellis (late forties) and Nigel Morant (early forties) who, having exhausted the subject under discussion, now wait impatiently for their mother to answer.

Annalise, however, concerned with how the issue affects certain preoccupations of her own (preoccupations she plans to divulge that evening), pays them scant attention.

NIGEL. Well? *(Beat.)* So, what do you say? *(Beat.)* Ma?
IMOGEN. Ma-a, it's late…!
ANNALISE. I'll think about it.
IMOGEN. What have you just been *doing?!* What's there to think *about?!*
NIGEL. Imogen's right. It's very simple. This man, Clayton —
IMOGEN. Leyton-Clarke.

NIGEL. — whatever, goes back to England —
IMOGEN. At the end of next week! Just see the man.
NIGEL. *(Crossing to pour himself a drink.)* It's for your benefit.
IMOGEN. Right! It's crazy not to!
ANNALISE. I said I'd think about it. *(She steels herself.)* But, as you're all here tonight, there's something I'd like to discuss b —
IMOGEN. *(Over the end of this.)* Hang on, Ma, can we deal with one thing at a time? Let's settle the painting first. It's the only chance you'll get. I know you'll regret it. Why are you so reluctant?? Is it a forgery or something? *(Kate Morant, late thirties, enters.)*
KATE. *(To Annalise.)* I've loaded the dishwasher
ANNALISE. Thank you, darling.
IMOGEN. *(To Annalise.)* Ja, and don't forget to turn it *on* this time.
ANNALISE. Thank you, darling.
IMOGEN. Yes, well … *["Remember last time? All the dishes went green?"]* Look, I can't stay here all night…! Reg'll be in a panic. He'll think something's happened to me.
KATE. Call him.
IMOGEN. *(Looks at Kate "It's a ploy, stupid.")* I don't want to wake the children. *(To Annalise.)* So what do you say?
ANNALISE. More tea, anyone?
IMOGEN. Ma-a!
ANNALISE. *(Getting up.) I* need some. *(She exits with her cup and the teapot.)*
IMOGEN. Well, think about it while you're there…! *(Nigel crosses to get a drink.)* God I hate this place!
KATE. Oh, Immie.
IMOGEN. Well, I *do.* Not *this,* the *area.* Though I never liked this much, either. It's much better since Reg knocked down that wall *(Her siblings exchange glances.)* and re-did the kitchen for her. Much nicer. Still. The area just gets worse and worse. She shouldn't *be* here now. I'm sorry but it's true.
KATE. No one's disagreeing.
IMOGEN. Yes, well, but I seem to be the only one who cares! And I've spoken till I'm blue in the face.
NIGEL. So has Christine.
KATE. She's not going to listen to Christine.
NIGEL. Why not?

KATE. ... No reason.
IMOGEN. She never listens to anyone.
NIGEL. Why don't *you* take her.
IMOGEN. *(Alarmed, defensive.)* What, home?
NIGEL. *(Indicating the painting.)* No. To — Clayton Layton.
IMOGEN. *(Calls.)* Ma-a...? Ma! Listen...! I can take y —
ANNALISE. *(Returning with her refilled teacup, stumbles, spilling some of the hot liquid on herself.)* Ow! Dammit! *(Her children dart forward.)*

IMOGEN.	KATE.	NIGEL.
Ma...!	Are you okay?	Did you burn yourself?

ANNALISE. *(It hurts. Something hurts. She impatiently wipes her clothes.)* I tripped. That's all. I'm fine.
KATE. Don't you w —
ANNALISE. I'm *fine,* thank you darling.
NIGEL. Imogen says she'll take you there. *(To Imogen.)* And bring you back.
IMOGEN. *(Defensive.)* Yes. Of course.
KATE. How's your ulcer these days?
ANNALISE. Fine! Touch wood.
IMOGEN. *(Consulting her diary.)* Wednesday afternoon, how's that?
ANNALISE. No, I'm seeing Dr. Goldman.
KATE. Oh?
ANNALISE. Just a check-up.
IMOGEN. Thursday, then. It's Dora's night off but we'll manage. Reg can fetch Freddie from Judo ... *(Kate and Nigel exchange looks.)* and Fiona. I'll have to cancel lunch; my massage; the dressmaker. And gym.
ANNALISE. *(Over the end of this.)* You don't want to do that.
IMOGEN. *(Hastily — and bravely magnanimous.)* Oh, I don't mind. So! I'll make the appointment, shall I? Reg'll cook us Chinese. Then he can drive you home. *(Annalise crosses to light a hurricane lamp near the painting.)* That's settled then. Thursday. Ma? Okay? Ma-a, I have to go! *(To the heavens.)* Ghorrr, sometimes I could strangle her ...

KATE.	NIGEL.
Immie ...	Relax.

IMOGEN. Yes, well, but I can't leave till I get an answer, can I?

Kate, for goodness sake, you talk to her. You're the only one she listens to…! Go on.
KATE. *(To Annalise.)* Wouldn't hurt.
IMOGEN. That's *right!*
KATE. Might be fun.
IMOGEN. Terrific fun. To know what it's worth. After all these years. Won't it?
KATE. You won't be obligated —

IMOGEN.	NIGEL.
Not at all.	No.

KATE. *(Pointedly.)* To anyone.

IMOGEN.	NIGEL.
Absolutely not.	Of course not.

KATE. *Least* of all us.
NIGEL. … Right! That's right!
IMOGEN. Imagine! If it's really valuable. I bet it is. They're especially looking for early ones.
ANNALISE. *(Jettisoning her original intentions.)* All right, yes, I'll go. But I don't need help, thank you, Imogen. I can go on my own.
IMOGEN. Okay. Fine! Yes. Of course, whatever you want. *(Fishes in her handbag.)* Here's the address. But you *will* go?
ANNALISE. *(Looking heavenwards.)* Oh my lord
IMOGEN. Not "oh my lord," will you go?

KATE.	ANNALISE.
Immie …	Yes, darling. I'll go…!

NIGEL. *(Polishes off his drink.)* Well! That was easy. *(He goes to get his jacket.)*
ANNALISE. You're leaving?
NIGEL. *(Kissing her.)* Have to, Ma.
ANNALISE. Oh! Just a minute. Wait. I've got something for you…! *(She exits to the kitchen.)*
IMOGEN. *(To Nigel.)* We'll see Kate home first. *(To Kate.)* Then you can return my necklace.
KATE. *Jawohl!*
IMOGEN. Very funny. *(To Nigel.)* She's had it for months…! Oh! Speaking of months — d'you know what Freddie said the other day? *(Kate and Nigel exchange a look.)* Reg was showing him a perpetual calendar — I must say Freddie got it, one, two, three —

then, he said to Reg: "Dad, when I was born you were thirty-four years older than me. But when I'm thirty-four, you'll only be twice as old." Isn't that amazing? How did he think of it!
KATE. Amazing.
IMOGEN. It was!
KATE. Can't your kids find their own way home? They're certainly old enough.
IMOGEN. You and Ma, you're both living in the past...! Don't you know what it's like out there? *(To Nigel.)* By the way, I hope you're following me to the turn-off. *(To Kate.)* You're away half the time. You have no idea. Mrs. Hastings was mugged ri — what am I saying "mugged"! People are getting *killed!* All over the place! Sally Hendrick's mother. Her car was hijacked. In broad daylight. They robbed her — and then they drove over her. And then they drove over her again, to make sure. And Sandy Emmet's dau —
NIGEL *(Over the end of this.)* Immie, don't trot out your list. We've all got a list.
IMOGEN. Yes, but she flits around the world with her "high-powered job," her www's, and she thinks it makes her an expert on everything. *(To Kate.)* You don't know the half!
NIGEL. Immie, for godsake ...
IMOGEN. *(Over this.)* It's mayhem! *(To Nigel.)* I'm sick of her hoity-toity ways. She doesn't live in the real world. *(To Kate.)* One in four houses has been broken into.
KATE. I don't pretend to be an expert, Imogen. You don't have to be. It's quite simple. It's chickens coming home to roost. *(Sometime during the following, unnoticed by her children, Annalise reappears. She listens a moment then, distressed, retreats.)*

NIGEL.	KATE.	IMOGEN.
Now hang, on Kate, it's not as easy as that. In fact a chap I know —	It's the truth, Nigel.	That's nonsense. Utter nonsense ... They've had five years for godsake...!
This chap s —	*(To Imogen.)* What's five years?! And who's this "they" *(To Nigel.)* You see — that's the kind of	
Ja, well, a chap tol —	attitu —	You're just like Ma...!

13

NIGEL.	KATE.	IMOGEN.
	I'm not saying it's great, Imogen. But compare it to what went before. *(To Nigel.)* Right?	
This cha —		*(To Nigel.)* She's just like Ma.
Face it, Immie, before it was just in the townships. Now it's all over the place. *(Loudly)* This chap I know … *(Breaks off.)* Ag, forget it…!	*(To Imogen.)* What would you do? If you had no job! *(To Nigel.)* Right? *(To Imogen.)* And no chance of one. *(To Nigel.)* Right?	
		Well, who's fault is th — What have they done in five years except line their own pockets. Reg, actually, Reg — Listen!
	I can't talk to her. *(To Imogen.)* I can't talk to you.	Do you know what the murder rate is? It's eight times higher than America. America!
She's right about that, Kate. No one's talking ab — *(Groans.)* Oh God, don't go over that old stuff about the hearings.	… D'you *know* how lucky we are?! Didn't anyone even listen to the hearings?? I bet not one of you even bo — … Nigel?! Sure. And they were just following orders…!	Oh please…! *(Dismissively.)* I did. Of course I did. We had no choice…! But those crimes are old. What about what's going on now! Rape and robbery's through the roof!
She's right, Kate.		Reg said there'd be violence. He's right.
	Nobody's disputing that, Imogen —	And it's rife with corruption…!
Hang on Immie, you can't compare this government with the white government bef — That's exactly what you're doing.	Course not!	I'm not doing that…! All I'm s — All I'm saying is

NIGEL.	KATE.	IMOGEN.
		things — Things have *never, ever* been this bad…!
	Well th — *["then"]*	
	Y — *["You know what?"]*	
	Then why don't you go…!	
It's not that easy, Kate …	Just leave.	*(With sarcasm.)* Oh, sure…!
	Yes it is.	I'll leave on Thursday.
	Dad was British.	
	Yes! Just get yourselves passports and *go* — or brush up on your Zulu…! *(She turns away, angry at herself as much as them.)*	You're absurd …

(Silence.)
IMOGEN. Well, anyway. *(Silence.)* At least she'll go. That's something. Reg never thought she would. Silence.
NIGEL. I keep looking round for Popeye.
KATE. Me, too. *(Annalise reenters.)*
NIGEL You should get another dog, Ma.
ANNALISE. I don't want another dog. I'd feel too disloyal to poor old Popeye.
NIGEL Well, I'm sure whoever poisoned him's delighted you feel that way. The coast's clear, now.
ANNALISE. Oh, rubbish. You know what an old scrounger he was. He found some bad meat, that's all. He wasn't in the best of health, in any case. *(Her children exchange grins.)*
KATE. Ma
IMOGEN. Unbelievable!
ANNALISE. Oh nonsense…! *(To Nigel.)* Here.
NIGEL. What's this?
ANNALISE. A milktart. My star pupil made it. *(The children glance at one another: Another burnt offering!)*
NIGEL. I can't. Christine's on one of her diets. She'd kill me.
ANNALISE. Well, little Ruthie will like it.
NIGEL. She would … But she's not allowed to eat sw —
KATE. *(To Nigel.)* For goodness sake. *(To Annalise.)* Give it to Imogen.

IMOGEN.	KATE.
Well, Ma, actually, no.	

15

IMOGEN.   KATE.
Reg has been told that he —   Great!
You know, he's got this —   Super! *I'll* take it! *(She takes it and gives Annalise a kiss.)* Thanks.

NIGEL. 'Bye, Mumsy! *(Kisses her.)* You're doing the right thing. *(He exits.)*
ANNALISE. *(Calling after him.)* Love to the family…!
IMOGEN. Don't go without us, Nigel! *(To Annalise and Kate, conspiratorially.)* Listen … I spoke to Christine the other day. She's very worried. She says they're retrenching at Chapman's. Nigel may lose his job. He's terribly upset. Don't say anything! He'd be furious if he thought you knew, you know what he's like. Anyway, it may not happen. I just thought you ought to know. If it did, I suppose he could work for Christine's dad.
KATE. He'd hate that.
IMOGEN. Yes, well, but what can one do? They live way above their means as it is. Anyway he's upset. *(She kisses the air next to her mother.)* Come along, Kate, I have to get home. No. Wait. I have to pee.
KATE. *(Staring open-mouthed after her sister.)* She's insufferable…!
ANNALISE. She means well. She likes to be involved, that's all.
KATE. Talk about living beyond your means! She's worse than Nigel. He's right, though. Ma, you should get another dog. I think he's planning to give you one.
ANNALISE. No. No. Absolutely not. You must stop him. No. *(As Kate starts to protest.)* Why do my children want to run my life…! I know I'm the wrong side of middle age but I'm not gaga! I'll tell you, for all your sister's gym and tennis and whatnot, I can still outwalk her. *(Beat.)* If you're like this when I'm of sound mind and body, what on earth will you be like when I'm ill?!
KATE. That's something to think about.
ANNALISE. Yes! *["isn't it!"]*
KATE. You couldn't stay here.
ANNALISE. Oh? Where would you have me go? Some ghastly walled-in retirement village? One of you? No offense, darling, but I've only just got rid of you! I've wanted to live by myself for years. I love it. Besides, look around, look at all my locks and bars! Thanks

to your sister and dear old Reg, I couldn't be safer! They even wanted to bar my skylight…! Thank God I won that argument…!
KATE. Okay.
ANNALISE. I live in Africa and I can hardly see the sun!
KATE. Okay. *(Annalise feels a stab of pain, which she conceals from her daughter.)* But do you still have Dad's old army gun?
ANNALISE. Yes.
KATE. I know you hate them. And it's probably useless but it's still a de — *["deterrent"]* Ma? Are you all right?
ANNALISE. Yes. I'm fine. *(Imogen enters carrying something. Annalise mouths, firmly: "I'm fine!")*
IMOGEN. This is a nice box. I've never seen it before. Fiona would love it. Can I take it for her?
ANNALISE. Where did you find that?
IMOGEN. In your bedroom.
ANNALISE. In my bedroom.
IMOGEN. On the chest of drawers. What's the matter?
ANNALISE. What w — *["were you doing in my bedroom?"]* Never mind.
IMOGEN. *(Looking inside.)* It's just a bunch of old photos and papers …
ANNALISE. *(In a burst of anger.)* No! D — Give me that…! *(She takes the box from her daughter and hugs it close.)*
IMOGEN. *(Startled.)* What's wrong?
KATE. For godsake, Imogen …
IMOGEN. *(Defensively.)* I'm just *looking!* Honestly! Anyone'd think they were state secrets! I'm *sorry,* okay? I just thought you might *like* to give it to your eldest grandchild.
ANNALISE. *(Dryly.)* Not just yet. *(She puts the box on her desk.)*
IMOGEN. Fine. Fine. That's fine. That's perfectly all right. Sorry I spoke. *(Hurt.)* It's not as though it's expensive or something. *(Beat, a failed attempt at lightness.)* Right, Katherine, let's go…! *(To Annalise, injured.)* Look after yourself, *["you silly old thing."]* *(To Kate.)* I'm not waiting.
ANNALISE. Best to Reg. Big hug to the children.
IMOGEN. *(Over her shoulder as she exits.)* Will do.
KATE. *(Gathering her things.)* Mommy, with all the palaver about the painting, you never said what it was you wanted to tell us.

ANNALISE. Oh, it was nothing. I just thought, as you were all here … But, it's fine. Another time. *(The car hooter sounds an irritable Morse code.)* Katie, when do you go to Lisbon?
KATE. Thursday.
ANNALISE. Oh … That's wonderful darling!
KATE. I'm back in a month.
ANNALISE. *(As long as that??)* Good. Good! Will … what's-his-name be there?
KATE. His name's Jean-Pierre.
ANNALISE. "Jean-Pierre."
KATE. Lisbon's strictly business.
ANNALISE. *(Teasingly skeptical.)* Oh?
KATE. It is! But I'll see him in Brussels afterwards.
ANNALISE. Will I ever meet him?
KATE. Mother, he's married.
ANNALISE. That makes him antisocial?
KATE. That makes it complicated. Besides, I thought you didn't approve.
ANNALISE. Did I say that?
KATE. Well — *["not in so many words, but"]* — *(The car hooter blares over this.)*
IMOGEN. *(Off.)* Kate, if you don't come now I'm going without you…!
KATE. I'll call you. *(Hugs her mother.)* Thanks for the tart.
ANNALISE. *(As Kate exits.)* Have fun in Lisbon…!

(Onstage:)	(Offstage:)
	IMOGEN.
(Annalise, checking the	I don't know why you
room, notes with	couldn't bring your own car …
concern how far the	NIGEL.
level in the brandy	She *told* you, Immie, it's
decanter has dropped.)	being fixed.
	IMOGEN.
	(Barreling on.) And seeing as you didn't, why you can't have more consideration for oth —
	KATE.
	Oh, Immie, shut up …

18

(Car doors close; cars start up.)
IMOGEN. *(Off. Calls.)* Stay inside, Ma…! Lock the door…!
ANNALISE. "Stay inside, Ma. Lock the door." *(Annalise picks up the tea tray. She stops in front of her painting and looks at it.)* You don't know the trouble you've caused…! *(She starts to exit, then turns back as:)*

Scene 2

Flashback.

1951. Slade River. The back garden of Julius van George's home.

A blazingly sunny day. The backdrop is Annalise's painting come to life — mountains, countryside (although the actual mountain is not in view).

A light-skinned Coloured man, Julius van George (in his early to mid thirties, not perhaps conventionally handsome, but his drive and air of self-possession make him immensely attractive) sits at his easel painting. An old radio sits on the stool near him. A path on the right leads to a rose garden. As he works, Young Annalise photographs him with her box camera. A basket of assorted vegetables lies on the ground in the near vicinity.

The older Annalise watches a moment before leaving the stage unobtrusively.

RADIO NEWSCASTER. *(Begun in the transition.)* … the Minister stated in Parliament that the blood transfusion service is a scandal. We are in danger of becoming a nation of Coloureds. He went on to say, it is not known what the biological reaction is when a person of one race is infected, or rather, he meant "injected" with the blood of someone from another racial group. Referring to the question of public hangings, the Minister of Justice said he is not prepared to reintroduce them. This is 1951, after all. It wouldn't be good for people to watch executions. Besides, *white* people are sometimes hanged and it would not be right if Natives and Coloured people were allow — *(Exasperated, van George turns off the radio.)*

YOUNG ANNALISE. Can you look here please? Smile. *(When he doesn't, compliantly:)* Okay. *(She clicks the shutter. A coloured woman (of indeterminate age — early to late thirties — enters carrying a basket filled with cut roses.)*

MARAAI. Miss Anna? Is this enough? Your Ma said I must pick a lot.

YOUNG ANNALISE. That's lovely, Maraai.

MARAAI. *(To van George.)* How much?

VAN GEORGE. Oh. *(Pulling a face.)* That *is* a lot.

MARAAI. How much?

VAN GEORGE. *(Deadpan.)* Ten shillings. *(He and Maraai are old sparring partners. Both enjoy it.)*

MARAAI. Allamapstieks! *["good gracious"]* Ten?! Ten?! For a bunch of old roses?! Nee! *["No"]* Nuhuh! In ten days they'll be dead! *(To Young Annalise.)* Your Ma didn't give me that kind of money. Nuhuh. Nee.

VAN GEORGE. Four.

MARAAI. Two. *(She nods.)* That's better…! *(Forks out the money:)* One. Two! For one little old bunch of roses … Gah! *(She crosses to sit on the grass.)*

YOUNG ANNALISE. Shouldn't you go home now, Maraai?

MARAAI. No.

YOUNG ANNALISE. Won't my Ma want the vegetables?

MARAAI. No, I can wait for Miss Anna.

YOUNG ANNALISE. Won't she be cross that I kept you out?

MARAAI. Nuhuh. I'll just sit here a little, in the sun.

YOUNG ANNALISE. *(A brainwave.)* I think my Ma would like some grapes. *(Maraai looks at her.)* I saw some hanepoot down by the gate. *(Pleadingly.)* Nice hanepoot…?

MARAAI. Aaag…! *(She gets to her feet.)* But Miss Anna can take her time. Okay? Take as long as Miss Anna likes.

YOUNG ANNALISE. Thanks, Maraai. *(Calls after her.)* Thank you…! *(Maraai exits. Young Annalise looks over at van George.)* … Right! *(He doesn't respond.)* I hope the photos come out. My camera has a mind of its own. *(Beat.)* I suppose there'll be one I can use. So! Let's begin. *(He continues working.)* It must be very satisfying to paint. To have that kind of skill.
VAN GEORGE. Don't you like journalism?
YOUNG ANNALISE. Oh, this is just a fill-in job…! My dad asked Mr. Fraser to take me on for the holidays. I like it. But I don't want to work for the Slade River *Gazette* all my life! I wouldn't get a job on a really big paper, I'm not qualified. My mom wants me to go back to college. For my teacher's diploma.
VAN GEORGE. Would you like that?
YOUNG ANNALISE. Look, this is the wrong way round. You're the one being interviewed.
VAN GEORGE. Quite right.
YOUNG ANNALISE. I do have shorthand. My Aunt Lily taught me.
VAN GEORGE. How is your Aunt Lily?
YOUNG ANNALISE. Fine.
VAN GEORGE. Still teaching music?
YOUNG ANNALISE. Yes, she's —
VAN GEORGE. Still driving her old Ford?
YOUNG ANNALISE. W — I think she — *I'm* supposed to ask *you* the questions.
VAN GEORGE. Ask away.
YOUNG ANNALISE. Okay…! So! *(Apologetically.)* It's only my second interview. And the first one wasn't a celebrity.
VAN GEORGE. Or a Coloured.
YOUNG ANNALISE. What?
VAN GEORGE. Isn't that why they sent you?
YOUNG ANNALISE. *(Amazed … angry … off-balance.)* … What?
VAN GEORGE. Forgive me, Miss Wynand. But isn't this an apt way to insult us both?
YOUNG ANNALISE. Wh — I — I don't *["know what you mean"]* —
VAN GEORGE. *(Over this.)* Insulting to you. To interview a Coloured.

YOUNG ANNALISE. I — No, I —
VAN GEORGE. Insulting to me. By sending not only an inexperienced junior but a temp?
YOUNG ANNALISE. I don — I — I'm not exac — !
VAN GEORGE. *(Over this.)* I don't mean to insult you in turn.
YOUNG ANNALISE. You — You did.
VAN GEORGE. *(Over this.)* If I did, I apologize.
YOUNG ANNALISE. *(Lost for words.)* ... Aren't you being a little over-sensitive? At least I'm white!
VAN GEORGE. *(Beat, he laughs.)* Yes, Miss Wynand. You are indeed white!
YOUNG ANNALISE. So it's not such an insult, is it? To you.
VAN GEORGE. *(Beat.)* Is it to you?
YOUNG ANNALISE. No. *(Pause.)* No, not at all.
VAN GEORGE. *(Beat.)* Well. *(Beat.)* So what is it you want to know, Miss Wynand?
YOUNG ANNALISE. ... Right! *(Consulting an aide-memoire in her notebook.)* ... Actually, I have to admit I don't know much about your work *(Realizes, and struggles on.)* — about art in general, so that's insulting, too.
VAN GEORGE. No. Practically no one in Slade River does know much about art. Certainly nothing about mine. As far as they're concerned, I'm a greengrocer. A Coloured gardener who lives too close to the village for their comfort.
YOUNG ANNALISE. I tried to find some of your paintings. I went to the li —
VAN GEORGE. *(Over the end of this.)* You won't. *(A touch of bitterness.)* What there is, is in private homes. In Cape Town. *(She writes this down.)* No, I'm wrong. Your Aunt Lily bought a painting once. *(She looks up, pleased.)* For three shillings. People pay more for my pumpkins than they do for my art.
YOUNG ANNALISE. Well, but maybe now that you've won?
VAN GEORGE. You think a prize will make the difference?
YOUNG ANNALISE. *(Beat.)* Wasn't there a row about it?
VAN GEORGE. A free-for-all! It's a prestigious prize. And a lot of money. The White community was scandalized that I won; the Coloured community was furious that I accepted. They say I'm a government stooge. *(She scribbles furiously.)* And a group of white

ladies — "The Women's Philanthropic Institute for Art" — petitioned the panel to take back the prize. They lost, I'm happy to say. I met all the entry qualifications. Next year I won't.
YOUNG ANNALISE. And what was the subject?
VAN GEORGE. *(Points.)* The Sleeping Beauty.
YOUNG ANNALISE. *(Gazing at it.)* She's wonderful, isn't she! We have a marvellous view from our garden … Oh! *(Eagerly.)* You know…! If you could paint her for me, I'd pay. More than three shillings. *(Beat, mortified.)* I don't mean to be insulting.
VAN GEORGE. You're not, Miss Wynand. I'd charge more than three shillings.
YOUNG ANNALISE. … Could you talk to me about painting?
VAN GEORGE. I don't exactly talk about it, I do it. *(Beat.)* I could show you. I could give you lessons.
YOUNG ANNALISE. *(Laughs.)* Me? I can't draw…! No, I meant tell me something about why you paint? What it means for you.
VAN GEORGE. Art, like morality, consists in drawing the line somewhere.
YOUNG ANNALISE. I like that. *(Repeating as she writes it down.)* "Art like mo …"
VAN GEORGE. Don't quote me!
YOUNG ANNALISE. Oh.
VAN GEORGE. I'm quoting someone else.
YOUNG ANNALISE. Oh. Who?
VAN GEORGE. Someone. *(She erases her jotting. And looks up, expectantly.)* Talk to you about painting…? Well, I suppose, in simple terms — no insult intended. For me, painting … it's not just technique, it's … With painting you have to see differently. You have to … to *listen* with your eyes. Look around you, Miss Wynand. See the tricks the light plays on our world, the transformations it creates! With light! Look. No, *look* at it! The most ordinary — *(He looks around.)* The basket. These roses. All illusion. Colour — what is it? It's light! And, you work backwards, you see, and brush stroke by brush stroke you build the colour. You create the light! You capture illusion with another illusion! Look at perspective! More illusion! But Art is more. Much more, it's … Wherever we look, we look for meaning. It's what we do, all of us. We have to do that, it's how we're built. And when you think of it! *(Gazes round the garden.)* All this…!

The Sleeping Beauty … The sky … The whole thing! Who could not paint? *(Suddenly feeling exposed.)* Anyway. You've come to the wrong man, Miss Wynand, I wouldn't know how to begin to tell you. *(Almost pedagogically.)* Of course you can't paint anything — not well — without technique.
YOUNG ANNALISE. *(Eagerly.)* Can you teach me some of that? *Could* you give me lessons? *(Maraai enters with the basket full of grapes.)*
MARAAI. Magtig. *["good God"] (Accusing van George.)* There's a lot of bees down there! Hooh! *(Suspiciously.)* How much?
VAN GEORGE. Nothing.
MARAAI. *["Nothing????"]* … Ag, no, Miss Anna must now help me! *(To van George.)* I can't just take the grapes.
VAN GEORGE. Why not?
MARAAI. Nee. Nuh-uh! *(With irrefutable logic.)* How can I pay nothing?
VAN GEORGE. Well, you've bankrupted me already.
MARAAI. *(A disbelieving laugh.)* Gahah…! *(Fishing in her pocket, she holds out two separate shillings.)* Dê! *["There."]* Take it. *(As he goes to take it, she withdraws her hand.)* Nuhuh. It's too much. *(Putting one of the coins back in her pocket, she hands him the other.)* One shilling *(She looks at him triumphantly.)*
VAN GEORGE. Thank you. *(Catching sight of his painting, Maraai studies it.)*
MARAAI. Huh! *["That's not bad!"] (She looks at him with a renewed respect.)* Huh! *["that's pretty good!"]*
VAN GEORGE. *(Acknowledging her high praise.)* Thank you. *(She strolls off to plonk herself down on "a patch of grass.")*
MARAAI. *(Magnanimously.)* Miss Anna can now carry on…!
YOUNG ANNALISE. Er — this'll sound silly, but do you have a picture of your painting?
VAN GEORGE. In the award ceremony's program. *(In Maraai's direction.)* My housegirl, Lena, knows where it is.
YOUNG ANNALISE. Maraai? *(Maraai lifts her eyes heavenward.)* The award ceremony's program? Can you get it for me please? *(Maraai gets up slowly. She looks at van George.)*
MARAAI. 'Your housegirl'?
YOUNG ANNALISE. … Maraai?

MARAAI. Ja, Miss Anna.
YOUNG ANNALISE. Do you mind…?
MARAAI. And if I did? *(Exiting.)* What would Miss Anna do…?
YOUNG ANNALISE. *(Calling after her.)* Thanks, Maraai. *(Beat.)* Thanks a lot…! *(She gazes after the departed Maraai for a moment. Then returns to van George.)* What will you do now?
VAN GEORGE. When the money comes, I'll leave. *(He begins to pack up his easel.)*
YOUNG ANNALISE. Leave Slade River?
VAN GEORGE. Leave the country.
YOUNG ANNALISE. … Where will you go?? I couldn't leave.
VAN GEORGE. Why should you?
YOUNG ANNALISE. I mean, I love Africa.
VAN GEORGE. So do I.
YOUNG ANNALISE. But, then, why?
VAN GEORGE. Laws, Miss Wynand. Every day more. And each law removes another right from the small handful that's mine. The Group Areas Act will soon be law. And I'm too close to the village for their comfort. I'll lose my house.
YOUNG ANNALISE. But it belongs to you.
VAN GEORGE. Not if they say it doesn't. We'll see when they draw their new zoning maps. While I've got the money, I'll go. My brother will keep things going for me. There isn't really a choice. I adapt much more and I kill my work. I don't and I'll end up in jail. *(He hands her a box.)* Pastels would be best for you. Three shillings an hour. Twice a week. *(During the scene change we hear the radio once more.)*
NEWSCASTER'S VOICE. Defending the "Group Areas Act" in Parliament yesterday, the Minister said racial zoning was not only necessary — some poor white people were now living in dreadful conditions — but we had only to look at the animal kingdom for confirmation of the Almighty's intention. Animals stick with their own kind. Applauding the Minister's comments this morning, Mr. Winterbotham of McKechnie-Burns and Company suggested that black workers on the factory floor be issued with coloured earmuffs, so as to further distinguish among different tribes. *(Fading out.)* Referring to the recent amendment to the Immorality Act, the Minister went on to say that …

Scene 3

A few days later. The office of an overseas firm of art dealers.

The lights come up on Annalise and Alistair Leyton-Clarke (an urbane Englishman anywhere from his late fifties into his seventies). Her painting is propped between them as, his business acumen at war with his aesthetic instincts, he studies it.

LEYTON-CLARKE. *(Keeping his enthusiasm in check as best he can.)* Yes … Yes … Well, Mrs. Morant, it certainly is a Julius van George…! And in tip-top condition. Early, of course.
ANNALISE. I thought y —
LEYTON-CLARKE. Which is what we're looking for…! Quite right … Not exactly a rare subject for him — *(Gazing at it avidly.)* the Sleeping Beauty mountain …
ANNALISE. *(With a laugh.)* No…!
LEYTON-CLARKE. You know his work then?
ANNALISE. Oh — er — no. *(Hastily.)* I do, but … *["only very slightly"] (Leyton-Clarke's eyes have strayed back to the painting.)*
LEYTON-CLARKE. Yes, well it's quite splendid — for an early work. And with the original frame. *(Gazing at it covetously.)* Superb colour perspective. Unlike those he did from memory. There's a spontaneity, a freshness. Obviously working direct from Nature.
ANNALISE. He was.
LEYTON-CLARKE. *["Oh??"]* One gains a lot from being *in situ*. Yes … The view is a little different. Interesting angle.
ANNALISE. It was done from our garden.
LEYTON-CLARKE. Slade River?
ANNALISE. My parent's home.
LEYTON-CLARKE. *(With quickened interest.)* You knew Julius then?
ANNALISE. … Everyone did, yes. He was the loc —

LEYTON-CLARKE. *(Dovetailing.)* Local greengrocer.
ANNALISE. I interviewed him for the village newspaper once.
LEYTON-CLARKE. You wouldn't, by any chance, have the certificate of sale?
ANNALISE. W — ... No.
LEYTON-CLARKE. Pity. A matter of provenance. *(She looks at him blankly.)* Verification. *(Hastily.)* Not that I doubt — No, no, not at all...! But documentation can help the price.
ANNALISE. Oh. Well, he — he gave it to me.
LEYTON-CLARKE. *["What??!"]* ... Did he?
ANNALISE. Yes, a ... A wedding present.
LEYTON-CLARKE. ... Most generous. *["This is not the Julius I knew."]* Yes indeed ... Mrs. Morant, may I ask ... Your parents ... What was your maiden name...?
ANNALISE. *(Beat.)* Wynand.
LEYTON-CLARKE. *(With a gleam of excitement, spelling.)* W-Y-N-A-N-D?
ANNALISE. Yes.
LEYTON-CLARKE. Good Lord. You're Annalise...!
ANNALISE. Yes.
LEYTON-CLARKE. Annalise Wynand! Well, well, well! I beg your pardon! It's — it's just that — Well, this is most unexpected...! Most. You may not know it, Mrs. Morant — no, of course you don't, how could you — but you've just solved a rather vexing question. Shortly after Mr. van George died, we found a small, unframed work, hidden among his papers. A pastel. Rough. Unfinished. And unusually abstract for Julius. Strange, rose petal clouds. *(Watching her.)* Your name was on the back. With a quotation.
ANNALISE. ... Yes, he was fond of those, I remember.
LEYTON-CLARKE. Wasn't he just! And enjoyed putting them on his work. Nothing very revelatory, of course, although they *(Watching her again.)* obviously meant something to him. And, clearly, they were private. Because, of course, once a painting is framed they're completely hidden. *(As she won't speak ... he nods.)* Private. Yes, an interesting man, Julius. He didn't let people in easily. I flatter myself I was among his few close friends. *(Caressing the frame in a proprietorial manner, reluctantly.)* I take it, then, you're

not inclined to sell …
ANNALISE. Oh no! No, no. *(Collects herself, in a more businesslike tone.)* No, I'm not.
LEYTON-CLARKE. *(Handling his disappointment admirably.)* Well, can't say I blame you…!
ANNALISE. My children thought I should get an appraisal. While I had the chance.
LEYTON-CLARKE. Absolutely. And I'm delighted to have seen it. *(Watching her.)* And, to meet the elusive "Annalise"! Well, I mustn't keep you. *(Goes to take the painting.)* I'll have someone wrap it, shall I?
ANNALISE. *(Intercepting him.)* No, no, I have something — *["outside"]*
LEYTON-CLARKE. Here *(Crossing to his desk.)*, let me give you my card. *(Charm personified.)* … And perhaps I'll get another chance. You never can tell … You know, I'd swear I've seen this painting before. Of course, he's done a number of Sleeping Beauty mountains, so it can be confusing. But I don't normally forget a painting. … Well, no matter.
ANNALISE. You said there was a quotation? On the back of the small — ?
LEYTON-CLARKE. *(Curious.)* The small pastel? Yes. Yes, the nineteenth century novelist, Jean-Paul Richter: "Remembrance is the only paradise out of which we cannot be driven away." *(He notices with curiosity the impact on Annalise.)* Yes … The work is a little damaged, I'm afraid, so not all that valuable. Well, pastels. A strange choice for Julius, because of course, except for one or two seascapes and a few minor watercolors, everything else was oils. *(Watching her.)* Wasn't it…?
ANNALISE. Oh, I lost track of Mr. van George … I married and moved up here to Jo'burg soon after he left the country. I haven't been back to Slade River in, oh, thirty years. No…! I've just remembered…! I loaned this to him once. For an exhibition. In London.
LEYTON-CLARKE. I knew I'd seen it before!
ANNALISE. I'm impressed…! It was a long time ago. 1960. *(Leyton-Clarke searches the back of the painting …)* That was the last time I saw him. I was in Slade River to take care of my mother. He came back out to pack up his house.

LEYTON-CLARKE. That's it, there's part of the old label...! Langford Gallery. That exhibition was his turning point. He just took off after that. And now, of course, since his death...! I must say we're rather disappointed. In spite of the publicity, very few paintings have come to light. Even in Cape Town. There are one or two possibilities ... I plan to come out again and twist some arms rather vigorously. Still, I did get to visit the "scene of the crime," so to speak. The house, of course, is quite gone.
ANNALISE. Oh...! Those beautiful roses ...
LEYTON-CLARKE. Oh, no no no. The rose garden is there. It's part of a public park. For the moment, at least. There's talk of some corporation buying the land.
ANNALISE. In Slade River...!
LEYTON-CLARKE. *(Shrugs.)* The way of the world ... But she's a beauty all right. I never realized. It's all there. Even the eyelashes...! *(They've warmed to each other.)*
ANNALISE. Yes, *(Pointing on the painting.)* It's a tree. It grows in the perfect place at just the right angle. My father was always afraid that "some blithering idiot" would chop it down. Or build a caravan park on her breasts. When I was little, he told me that we were the Sleeping Beauty's dreams — whatever we did was what she dreamed we did.
LEYTON-CLARKE. What a nightmare...!
ANNALISE. Yes! Julius said she was Africa. And when, one day, she awoke, we'd all be irrelevant — he meant whites, of course — we'd be irrelevant.
LEYTON-CLARKE. D'you know, that reminds me of when I w — *(The telephone rings.)* Excuse me. *(Answers.)* Leyton-Clarke. Charles...! Did you get it? ... What? *(A setback.)* Oh. I see. *(He listens intently, a frown on his face.)* ... Well, perhaps we should offer them — Yes! ... Do it! I don't care, whatever it takes ... Yes. Yes. And Charles, I'll be there...! *(He replaces receiver, beat, he turns to Annalise.)* Unavoidable business, I'm afraid. Delighted to have met you Miss Wyn — Mrs. Morant. And perhaps the next time I'm over...? May I call you?
ANNALISE. Yes, I —
LEYTON-CLARKE. Good. Excellent!
ANNALISE. — I don't believe you mentioned ...

LEYTON-CLARKE. Oh, of course! Er … *(Studying the painting.)* let me see … There's quite a demand for his early work. And the unique view gives it a rather special value. I'd say … My conservative guess is … In the region of two hundred and forty. *(She looks at him blankly.)* Pounds sterling.
ANNALISE. *(Trying to conceal her disappointment.)* Two hundred and forty pounds.
LEYTON-CLARKE. Oh good Lord no! *Thousand.* Two hundred and forty thousand pounds. *(Annalise stares at him, stunned. As the lights fade:)* Yes, well, I'll see you out then, shall I? *(Firmly.)* No no, I'll carry this. *(In the scene change, we hear the telephone ring. An answering machine picks up.)*
ANNALISE'S VOICE. Morant residence. Please leave a message.
ALISON'S VOICE. Mrs. Morant, this is Dr. Goldman's surgery again. It's about your tests. Doctor would like to see you as soon as possible. Thank you. *(Leyton-Clarke reenters [into some limbo area]. He takes out his cellular phone, dials.)*
LEYTON-CLARKE. … Alistair Leyton-Clarke, Mrs. Morant. Something interesting has come up in Zimbabwe with regard to another artist, Joshua Mkwayi. Fascinating work. So I'm extending my stay. I wondered if you'd care to have dinner with me next Friday. Would you ring me at my office when you get this message? Look forward to hearing from you. *(His opening gambit launched, he nods to himself and, with a satisfied smile, returns the phone to his pocket.)*

Scene 4

Annalise's living room. At the tail end of the day.

Annalise is busy going through the contents of an old cardboard packing crate. A number of books already litter the floor along with sundry other items (a few dilapidated toys, keepsakes from the past), including an old easel.

ANNALISE. … Please, darling, don't be cross. I haven't insured it all these years. I'm not going to start now. I simply can't afford it. Are you listening, Nigel?
NIGEL. *(Pouring himself a drink.)* Yes.
ANNALISE. What are you doing?
NIGEL. I'm listening.
ANNALISE. I'm not changing my attitude just because some art dealer puts a different value on it.
NIGEL. It's not that simple, Ma. It's not just "a different value." It's one hundred and twenty thousand pounds. Isn't that what you said?
ANNALISE. Yes.
NIGEL. One hundred and twenty thousand pounds! For one painting. Do you know what that is in *rands*?
ANNALISE. Ni —
NIGEL. It's a fortune! It changes things, Ma. *(Quickly.)* For *you*. It changes everything.
ANNALISE. It changes nothing. Not a thing. *(She gets up, leans the easel against the desk.)* It has the same value for me it's always had. And it's staying right on this wall, where it's always been and where no one but me has bothered with it for years. *(Crossing to the hurricane lamp.)* I won't treat it any differently. I certainly won't pay some corporation a vast sum of money I can't afford. *(Answering his implied desire.)* And I've no intention of selling.
NIGEL. Ma, what are you doing? You're not lighting that lamp?! You can't *do* that anymore!

ANNALISE. I've been doing it for years.
NIGEL. What if there's an accident?
ANNALISE. *(Sharply.)* I don't plan to *have* one!
NIGEL. That's why they're called accidents…! Okay. Forget it. Just forget the painting. Imogen's right, it's no use telling you what to do. You'll do exactly what you want. You always do. I just think it's a little irresponsible — not to mention unnecessary — in this day and age, to be lighting that kind of lamp.
ANNALISE. I grew up — ! *["up with them!"]* I don't want to argue, darling, I've already had two sermons from Imogen and I'm just a teeny bit tired.
NIGEL. *(Alert, suspicious.)* What did she say?
ANNALISE. More or less the same things.
NIGEL. *(Pouring another drink.)* What exactly?
ANNALISE. I don't know, "Reg says they'll pay for the insurance. Reg says they'll store the painting for me. In their house. That way Reg can keep it under *his* insurance."
NIGEL. I hope you said "no" on all counts.
ANNALISE. Ni —
NIGEL. You did say "no"?
ANNALISE. Of course I did. Can we talk about something else? I don't know where those books are.
NIGEL. What books? Oh. Well, don't worry about it.
ANNALISE. I thought it was important? Isn't that why you came to see me? Ruthie needs them for a school project?
NIGEL. Well, she'll just have to use something else. If you can't find them, you can't find them. *(Guilty.)* Here. I'll do that, Ma. You sit down.
ANNALISE. Thank you darling. *(Crossing to her desk.)* Thank you. *(He sets about repacking. Annalise's eyes light on the little box that Imogen coveted in Scene 1. She picks it up …)* How's Christine…?
NIGEL. She's fine. She sends her love. *(Going through the contents of the box.)*
ANNALISE. Give her mine.
NIGEL. Actually she's *not* feeling so well. The pregnancy's getting her down. *(Finding an old blue sheet of paper, she unfolds it. She reads the name …)*
ANNALISE. Well, it's not long now.

NIGEL. No. Then there'll be four of us ... What's that?
ANNALISE. Why is everyone so snoopy?!
NIGEL. Ma, it's the first t — *["time I've seen it"]*
ANNALISE. *(Over this.)* It's nothing. It's just some old papers. Photographs ... Some of Daddy's old things ... *(Putting the box aside.)* Nothing. *(She places the blue paper next to the telephone.)* It's nice to see you twice in ten days.
NIGEL. *(Defensively.)* What's that supposed to mean?
ANNALISE. It's nice to see you, Nigel. *(Beat.)* How are things at Chapmans?
NIGEL. Has Christine been talking to you?
ANNALISE. No, I — The last time we spoke, you were up for promotion.
NIGEL. Well, things have changed since then.
ANNALISE. *(Sympathetically.)* Have they?
NIGEL. Ma, the whole country's in the doldrums, what do you expect? Chapman's is lousy. It's *all* lousy as a matter of fact.
ANNALISE. I'm sorry, darling.
NIGEL. *(Trying to keep the desperation out of his voice.)* Well, we'll manage, I suppose. We always do. *(Changing tack, "head of the family" now.)* Ma, I want you to listen to me. I think it's time to move.
ANNALISE. *(She knows he means her.)* Why would you want to do that? You've just said th —
NIGEL. *(Over the end of this.) You*, Ma. Time for *you* to move. Especially now. Face it, the neighborhood's unrecognizable.
ANNALISE. Really? That's the best news I've had in years!
NIGEL. You can't go out at night.
ANNALISE. I don't want to. I'm perfectly happy with a telephone.
NIGEL. *(Snorts.)* When you *answer* it. *(He picks up the easel.)*
ANNALISE. Ah, except Friday...! *(Pleased.)* I'm going out Friday.
NIGEL. *(Instantly suspicious.)* Oh?
ANNALISE. Just dinner. No one you know. *(He goes to place the easel back in the box.)* No, don't p — Leave that out.
NIGEL. You going to start painting again?
ANNALISE. I might. *(He sets the easel down and comes over to her.)*
NIGEL. Look, Ma, I'm not saying there's anything wrong with the neighborhood *per se.*

ANNALISE. Oh, Nigel, do stop!
NIGEL. *(Over the end of this.)* But, in certain situations, there's a ripple effect.
ANNALISE. *(Over the end of this.)* I've not the slightest intention of moving!
NIGEL. *(Over the end of this.)* Things no one can control! *Friends* of friends. That sort of thing.
ANNALISE. I heard this all from Imogen an hour ago…!
NIGEL. Because we worry about you…! Face it, you never liked it!
ANNALISE. I loathed it! I'm delighted it's changed. I only hope they're not just darker versions of the people before…! Nigel, d'you remember? Remember when we first came here…?
NIGEL. Ma. I was two.
ANNALISE. It was so different then…! Recognizably Africa. Five or six houses, that's all. Open veldt, koppies. Wide wide skies. You could walk for miles. Then little by little … Well, like most things, I suppose. By the time you realize what's happening, it's happened. Then your father died.
NIGEL. *(Dryly.)* He didn't do it deliberately.
ANNALISE. No. All the same, we were trapped. Marooned in this circumscribed, trivial little place …
NIGEL. Yes, so that's all the m —
ANNALISE. *(Over this.)* And I know Imogen resents me bitterly for selling Grannie's jewelry. And all the other stuff. *(On a roll.)* I suppose it would've been nice to pass it on. To the three of you. But at the time, I thought it would let me give you some options. A better life!
NIGEL. *(Who has been trying to say something, finally gets out:)* Ma.
ANNALISE. *(Over this.)* I think I honored my obligations, Nigel. To all three of you. I honoured my obligations — the best way I knew! Why do I feel you both want me to be guilty! You could have gone to university.
NIGEL. *(With a groan.)* Ma —
ANNALISE. Yes! After the army. You could have!
NIGEL. Don't go over that old ground…!
ANNALISE. Yes, well, this afternoon Imogen nearly buried me in "that old ground!" Dumped it all over me. It's so funny, I spent my whole life wanting to get away from this place and now when I'm

finally beginning to quite like it, you're all nagging me to leave...! And I know none of you thinks much of my work. You're right. It *isn't* much — *(Self-mocking.)* "volunteer cooking instructor at a vocational school" — but it's something useful...!

NIGEL. Imogen just feels they should pay you. *Something*. For all the hours you do. And if you want *my* opinion. I thin —

ANNALISE. Where's the money coming from, Nigel? They don't have the money! Isn't it time to give a little back?

NIGEL. For crying out loud ...

ANNALISE. Nigel —

NIGEL. I understand! I do. I promise. I understand! *(He stares at her ...)* I know what you think, Ma. I know what you think of me. *(... She opens her mouth to speak.)* No, no. No, you do. You do. It's okay *["it's not"]*, I'm used to it.

ANNALISE. What are you *talking* about?

NIGEL. *(Over this.)* But we're different, Ma. Everyone's different!

ANNALISE. Nig —

NIGEL. Yes! Yes, and it's not the whole story! Believe me! There are things you don't know, Ma! You don't know the *half* of it...! And if I'd done, been, everything *you* wanted me to — that you never could! — I'd have been arrested years ago...! Worse!

ANNALISE. Nig —

NIGEL. *(Over this.)* Just let me have my own opinions! *(Beat, as she goes to speak.)* My own opinions! Please! *(Beat.)* My own opinions. *(Pause.)*

ANNALISE. You're right. I'm sorry, darling. *(She goes to touch him but he draws back out of reach.)* It doesn't pay to look back. One sees only one's mistakes.

NIGEL. *(Raising his hands and eyes heavenwards. To himself.)* Mistakes...!

ANNALISE. We none of us did anything. Practically nothing! *[She means herself]* How feeble we were!

NIGEL. ... I have to go. *(He grabs up the box. Exiting the room.)* I really, *really* have to go ...

ANNALISE. *(Staring blankly ahead of her.)* How *weak* ... *(He reenters boiling — trying to keep it under control.)*

NIGEL. Ma ... Let me ask you something. *(Grabbing up his jacket.)* Out of curiosity. May I?

ANNALISE. Of course.
NIGEL. *(Putting on his jacket.)* If you'd known, years ago, what the painting was worth. Would you have sold it? To "give us a better life"? Would you have done that? *(She stares at him in dismay.)* You don't have to answer now. Think about it. Just think about it. Okay? ... *(Mutters.)* Got to go. *(Over his shoulder.)* Look after yourself. I'll lock up.
ANNALISE. *(Stricken.)* G'bye. *(Annalise remains where she is for a moment, trying to marshall her thoughts, her emotions. Then, coming to a decision, she crosses to the telephone, removes the piece of blue paper. She looks at the name a moment then, grabbing the Yellow Pages, she flicks through them, rapidly. She selects a number, checks her watch, then dials. We hear the dialing and the ring on the speakerphone.)*
JOYCE'S VOICE. *(Bright, very friendly.)* Hello. *(Annalise, about to speak, realizes it's a recorded message.)* This is the "I Spy" Detective Agency — experts in surveillance. Electronic bugging. *De*bugging. All tracing services: lost spouses; parental abductions; long or short-term missing persons. Matrimonial and other indiscretions, all photographs tastefully executed. Experts in art fraud. *(Annalise turns back to the phone.)* And art forgeries. No job is too difficult. Everything is strictly confidential. Our offices are closed right now, please call back Mondays to Fridays between eight-thirty A.M. and 4:30 P.M. *(Annalise replaces the receiver. She returns the blue paper to its box ... She switches off the light at her chair, only the hurricane lamp burns, very low. She leans back, lost in thought. A figure appears ...)*

Scene 5

Flashback.

Early 1952. Slade River. The garden belonging to the Wynand family. Dawn.

Young Annalise emerges from the shadows upstage (she crosses the living room past the older Annalise in the chair) glancing back as if afraid of being seen or followed. She paces anxiously, expectantly. Maraai comes up the path.

YOUNG ANNALISE. *(Coming forward.)* Maraai. *(Maraai lets out a shriek, Young Annalise quickly hushes her.)*
MARAAI. O hete! *["Oh jeez!"]* Miss Anna gave me such a fright! *(Noting Young Annalise's caution, she lowers her voice automatically.)* Why's Miss Anna up so early?
Young Annalise. *(Drawing Maraai D.)* I want to talk to you.
Maraai. *(Instantly suspicious.)* Me?? What's the matter, Miss Anna? What have I done?
YOUNG ANNALISE. No, nothing…! … I — I'm going away, Maraai.
MARAAI. Hey? Why? Where? Does your Ma know?
YOUNG ANNALISE. Everyone knows. I'm going to Cape Town.
MARAAI. Cape Town! Back to college? *(Breaking into a happy smile.)* Ag, I'm so glad! Oooh, lekker, lekker! *["lovely, lovely"]* *(Young Annalise hushes her again.)* Your Ma must be happy, nê? *["not so?"]* Ag, shame, she always wanted you to go back. *(Noticing Young Annalise's demeanor.)* What's wrong?
YOUNG ANNALISE. I need you to do something for me.
MARAAI. … Me?
YOUNG ANNALISE. Yes.
MARAAI. What?
YOUNG ANNALISE. Something important. A favor.

MARAAI. A favor? *["this means trouble"]*
YOUNG ANNALISE. And you have to keep it secret.
MARAAI. Nuhuh … No … *(Backing away.)* No, Miss Anna. Nuhuh.
YOUNG ANNALISE. Wait …
MARAAI. Nee, nuhuh —
YOUNG ANNALISE. *(Over this.)* Just wait — !
MARAAI. *(Over this.)* Miss Anna can't *do* that to me.
YOUNG ANNALISE. I'm not doing anything to you…! I just need your help.
MARAAI. But I can't —
YOUNG ANNALISE. *(Over this.)* You won't get into trouble, I promise.
MARAAI. Huh!
YOUNG ANNALISE. *(Over this, desperate now, close to tears.)* You won't! Not if you keep quiet. I promise…!
MARAAI. *(Shaking her head.)* Miss Anna, your Ma —
YOUNG ANNALISE. Just listen! Please! *(Maraai looks at Young Annalise.)* Please, Maraai. *(Maraai sighs, heavily.)* You can say no if you like. *(Maraai flashes her a look of disbelief.)* You can. I promise. Okay? Just — Come and sit down. Okay? Please.
MARAAI. A-a-ag…! What's Miss Anna done now? *(Young Annalise takes her hand. Reluctantly Maraai lets herself be led off. They exit. The light shines dimly on Annalise in her chair … From somewhere outside we hear voices …)*

Scene 6

Annalise's living room, moments later.

The voices coming from outside her window interrupt Annalise's reverie (it takes a moment for her to locate them). Frozen with fear, she listens.

VOICE 1. *(Off.)* Yo! Re mo kae? *["Where are we?"]*
VOICE 2. *(Off.)* Ga ke tsebe. *["I don't know"]*
VOICE 1. *(Off.)* Eh! Ntlo e ke ya ga mang?! *["Whose house is this?"]* Heh? Motho yole ke mang? *["Who is this?"]* *(The doorbell rings.)*
VOICE 2. I don't know! Tshipi? *["Tshipi?"]* O a mo tseba na? *["Do you know this person?"]* *(Fighting down her fear, Annalise slowly, quietly gets to her feet.)*
VOICE 3. *(Off.)* Éê! Mosadi wa lekgowa. *["Yes. It's a white woman"]*
VOICE 1. *(Off.)* Yo, yo, yo, yo, yo …
VOICE 3. *(Off.)* Thula! *["Shut up"]* *(The doorbell rings again.)* Mrs. Morant. *(Annalise stops, startled at hearing her name.)*
VOICE 1. *(Off.)* Hau! A motho wa mogolo! *["Oh! Poor woman"]* *(There's the sound of suppressed laughter. She crosses to the desk, opens a drawer, takes out a gun, handling it like an alien object.)*
VOICE 2. *(Off.)* Bua Sentle. O se kê wa bua thota. *["Speak nicely. Don't say too much"]*
VOICE 3. *(Off. Calls.)* Mrs. Morant?
ANNALISE. Who is it? Who's there?
VOICE 3. *(Off.)* Tshipi.
ANNALISE. Who?
VOICE 3. *(Off.)* Tshipi.
ANNALISE. I'm sorry, I don —
VOICE 3. *(Off.)* Hau! My mother worked for you.
ANNALISE. Your mother?
VOICE 3. *(Off.)* Lulu.
ANNALISE. … You're *Lulu's* son?? And *what's* your name??

VOICE 1. *(Off.)* Mmolêlêlê, maan! *["Tell her!"]*
VOICE 3. *(Off.)* Nnyaa! *["No."] (Calls.)* It's Tshipi. *(Gun in hand, she stands frozen, listening.)*
VOICE 2. *(Off.)* Heh! Yo! Ke hatsetse. *["I'm cold"]* I'm going. *(Retreating.)* Ga ke rate molato *["I don't want trouble"]*, Tshipi.
VOICE 1. *(Off.)* Éê. *["Yes"] (Further away.)* Nkêmêlê. *["wait for me"]*
VOICE 2. *(Off. Further away.)* Hayikona! *["No way!"]*
VOICE 3. *(Off.)* Mrs. Morant. *(Pause.)* My name before was Gregory.
ANNALISE. ... Gregory? *(Silence.)* Is that you?
VOICE 3. *(Off.)* Éê. *["Yes"]* But now I'm Tshipi.
ANNALISE. I see. Who's with you, Gr — Tshipi?
VOICE 3. *(Off.)* Some other people. *(Beat.)* They are waiting in the car. I want to speak with you.
ANNALISE. It's late, Tshipi. I was going to bed. Can you come round tomorrow?
VOICE 3. *(Off.)* Gwa bo go reng ka wena! *["Damn, what's the matter with her!"]*
ANNALISE. What?
VOICE 3. *(Off.)* Can you let me in?
ANNALISE. Are you in trouble?
VOICE 3. *(Off.)* Hau! I want to *talk* with you! *(Remembering the formula.)* Please.
ANNALISE. ... Well, I... First, I have to ask you some questions. All right? *(Beat.)* I'm sorry to do this but I can't open the door unless I'm sure it's you. I hope you understand. Okay? *(Beat.)* Okay. Do you remember my children's names?
VOICE 3. *(Off.)* Yes.
ANNALISE. *(Waiting to hear them.)* Yes?
VOICE 3. *(Off.)* Yes! *(Pause.)*
ANNALISE. And my husband's? And my dog's name?
VOICE 3. *(Off.)* Seeleele... *["this is stupid...!"]*
ANNALISE. What's my son's name?
VOICE 3. *(Off.)* Nigel. And Kate and Imogen. And the dog is Popeye. Your husband I don't remember. He was dead. *(Pause.)* Mrs. Morant.
ANNALISE. Are you still alone?
VOICE 3. *(Off.)* Yes.

ANNALISE. All right. *(She weighs the question of the gun. Looking round, she settles on putting it behind the cushion on her chair.)* Just a minute… Just a minute. I'll be there… I'm coming. *(She goes to the door. And comes face to face with an African in his early twenties.)* Oh! Oh, Greg — Tshipi…! I — wouldn't have recognized you! How many years has it been? About eleven, yes? Goodness! *(Deliberately holding out her hand.)* It's nice to see you again. *(After a second, he shakes it perfunctorily.)* Come and sit down. Something to drink? *(He remains standing, glancing round the room. Trying not to show her nervousness, she sits.)* How's your mother? Is she okay? I haven't seen her in a long time. Where is she living, now?
TSHIPI. Soweto.
ANNALISE. Has she started work again?
TSHIPI. She doesn't work any more.
ANNALISE. Uhuh. *(With as much charm as she can muster.)* Sit down, please. Please. *(He perches on the edge of a seat.)* So! What can I do for you? *(The telephone shrills out. Tshipi springs to his feet.)* Excuse me. *(He comes to stand near her as she answers.)* Hello? …Imogen — can I call you back? I'm busy right now. *(Firmly.)* I'll call you back *(She replaces the receiver.)*
TSHIPI. Can you lend me some money?
ANNALISE. Are you in trouble?
TSHIPI. I need some money.
ANNALISE. How much?
TSHIPI. A hundred rand. *(She gets up and crosses to her desk.)* Two hundred. I need two hundred rand. *(Opening the secret drawer, Annalise removes some notes. She counts out R200. She holds it out, both are aware there is money over.)*
ANNALISE. Two hundred. *(He takes it. We sense the intense relief flooding through him. Knowing it's not part of the tacit agreement but feeling it's important to say.)* There's no rush. Pay it back when you can. *(Clutching the leftover notes, she crosses back to her chair.)* So, how are things with you otherwise? What are you doing now?
TSHIPI. I'm working.
ANNALISE. Oh…? Good. There's not much work around these days, is there. For anyone. I'm teaching again, part-time. *(Smiles.)* At your old school. Do you remember when I first took you there? I have the photograph somewhere…! *(He's edging towards the door,*

eager to leave.) Yes, well ... A lot has happened since then. Hasn't it. *(She notices him glance around the room again. She smiles.)* But nothing much has changed in here. *(At the entrance, he hesitates. They look at each other.)* Well. Ask your mother to come and visit me, will you? Gregory? I'd really like to see her again.
TSHIPI. It's Tshipi.
ANNALISE. Tshipi. Yes. *(Beat.)* Yes. Well. Goodbye. *(She holds out her hand. He checks his impulse to take it, half nods an acknowledgment — a 'thank you' — then turns and leaves. As Annalise struggles with her emotions, we hear a car engine start up; a car pulls off. The telephone rings. When the answering machine responds, a light comes up on Imogen in a limbo area, D., wearing a dressing-gown.)*
IMOGEN.
It's me, Ma. It's Imogen.
(Beat.) Pick up Ma.

(Annalise reenters.

Ma, pick up. Well. Okay.
Listen. It's late, we're going to bed.   *She goes over to her music*
I just wanted to say — Well, ring me   *system and turns it on.*
tomor — No. Wait. On *second* thoughts ...
This is a good chance to talk without   *She removes the gun from*
being interrupted...! But ring me when   *behind the cushion, returns*
you get this, I need to know you're all   *it to the desk drawer.*
right. The thing is, Reg and I have   *Then, crossing back to the*
been talking, and Reg thinks — we   *radio, she turns it up. High.*
both think — that the best thing ...   *She exits.)*

(The lights fade. The light remains on Imogen. She continues to talk. We know because we watch her gesticulating, and we see her lips move. But, barring a few key phrases (e.g. "that skylight"; "Reg says ... " "dangerous"; "Reg also ..."; "Reg's lawyer"; "safeguarding it"; "Nigel called me"; "honestly"; "listens to a word I say...!"), the music takes over, drowning her out.)
IMOGEN. *(Speaking as long as needed to cover Annalise's quick change.)* ... the best thing, under the circumstances, because of the painting of course, the best thing for all concerned would be to bar that skylight. Now I know you don't want that, but Reg says it's just too dangerous. So I think you're going to have to accept it, Ma. In the end. If you leave the painting there. Reg also feels that,

since you don't want *us* to look after it, Reg's lawyer would be the best person to consult about safeguarding it. He can advise on the legal ramifications. You don't have to *do* anything, Ma, just speak to him. Oh, Nigel called me a little while ago, he seemed upset about something. Goodness knows, I just have all our interests at heart. I, honestly, I sometimes feel that nobody in this family ever listens to a word I say...! *(The lights cross fade, coming up on:)*

Scene 7

Alistair Leyton-Clarke's office in Johannesburg. Friday evening.

The lights come up on Leyton-Clarke and Annalise in the middle of a lively discussion. On the table are: a carafe of water with a glass over the top, an open bottle of wine (half-empty), two half-empty glasses, two small plates with the remains of food on them, cocktail napkins, a larger plate of canapés, another of crudités or similar

Annalise has been glancing through a glossy catalogue.

ANNALISE. ... I suppose it's my — totally outdated — opinion that art should have some *aesthetic* component!
LEYTON-CLARKE. You sound like my late wife.
ANNALISE. Do I? Well, but really, Alistair, *(Indicating the catalogue.)* some of this ... postmodern stuff. It's a load of old rubbish!
LEYTON-CLARKE. *(Pointing to the opposite page.)* Literally.
ANNALISE. Yes! But then, you see, it's "blessed" by a High Priest of Art and suddenly, it's sacred...! The humble wafer becomes "the Body of Christ."
LEYTON-CLARKE. Which the faithful swallow — so to speak. Yes, I suppose in today's market the purchase of any work is an act of faith. But, it's not just anyone's blessing, Annalise. The high priests may not be "anointed" but they are "appointed."

ANNALISE. I've offended you.
LEYTON-CLARKE. Not at all...! My tastes are conservative. *(Taking the catalogue, a shade defensively.)* This fellow sells a lot of work...!
ANNALISE. And good luck to him! I don' — *(She winces with pain, it's stronger than previously.)*
LEYTON-CLARKE. *(Coming to her aid.)* Is something wrong?
ANNALISE. ... No, no ... It's nothing. *(Fishing in her bag.)* My ulcer. I have some pills. *(Leyton-Clarke hands her some water, she swallows the pill with some ad-libbing: "I'm sorry." "Don't apologize." "I'm fine now." "Another sip.")* Thank you. I'm fine. really I am. Thank you. *(Deflecting attention.)* Tell me, Alistair, I'm curious, is my painting really worth that much?
LEYTON-CLARKE. *(His dealer instincts to the fore.)* Ah, well, that depends. Possibly more. For instance, knowing the provenance *(Answering her blank stare.)* — the story behind it — could add to its value. Considerably. That's something to think about.
ANNALISE. *(Smiles.)* But I'm not selling.
LEYTON-CLARKE. No, no, no, of course you're not. But, if you were. People pay for that.
ANNALISE. *(A sudden thought.)* Is this why we're here? To try and — *["pressure me to sell?"]*
LEYTON-CLARKE. Oh my dear...! No. Not at all!! Not at all. No. No. No. Perish the thought...!
ANNALISE. I certainly will...!
LEYTON-CLARKE. No, it's only that we had a calamitous incident with a painting going astray, so I receive all shipments personally now. It shouldn't take long. I hope you don't mind.
ANNALISE. *(Shakes her head.)* I'm having fun!
LEYTON-CLARKE. So am I! Remarkable fun. *(She proffers her wine glass. He pours them both more wine with some ad-lib: "Should you be having this?" "Oh yes. Just a little.")* So what happened in the end? *(She looks at him, blankly.)* With the young man — er — ?
ANNALISE. Tshipi? That's all really. He left.
LEYTON-CLARKE. What did your children have to say?
ANNALISE. Oh, I wouldn't tell them...! It's just the ammunition they need.
LEYTON-CLARKE. You don't confide in them then?

ANNALISE. *(Smiles.)* They say I'm secretive. Stubborn and secretive…! They're right. I've told you more tonight than I've told anyone in years…!
LEYTON-CLARKE. And it's not even dinner time.
ANNALISE. I don't know what's come over me.
LEYTON-CLARKE. I'm flattered. Hope it's not just the wine.
ANNALISE. *(Smiles.)* It's a sad commentary on my life that I think Tshipi's visit's such a memorable event. You know, afterwards, I felt quite … well, *foolish*, for one.
LEYTON-CLARKE. I'd say it was a not-so-subtle form of mugging.
ANNALISE. *(Surprised.)* … Oh? No, I don't think so. It's not that simple. Tshipi's generation … they've been left out in the shuffle … Lost. The very ones who fought for change. We've been so lucky, Alistair. It could have been so different. I marvel at it. Living our sheltered, blinkered lives. And the things that were done in our name…! So many mistakes. *(Beat.)* You see, with Tshipi … I'm not responsible for his life, I'm not, but I am for my own. And from the time he was two until he was eight, my house was Tshipi's home. He lived there with his mother. I was involved with that little boy. And we are responsible for our involvements. Don't you think? We are.
LEYTON-CLARKE. *(Responding to something sensed beyond the spoken.)* My father was a captain in the war. He said, in some situations — he meant war — it was utterly unimportant *why* people behaved the way they did. *How* they behaved was all that mattered — as for *who*, that was unpredictable. And often quite surprising! But behaving better, *made* you so. Those who acted bravely, became *braver*. And the reverse, of course.
ANNALISE. … Yes. Why did you say that?
LEYTON-CLARKE. I don't know. It seemed appropriate.
ANNALISE. My Kate was especially fond of little Gregory. Tshipi. Very protective. I remember, when she was ten — he was barely three — she took him to the public playground on the corner. She was pushing him on the swing. Some neighbourhood children came. They knocked him off. It was a White park, of course, Katie didn't think of that. There was a terrible row. The children were shouting. Little Gregory was crying, quite bewildered by this gratuitous bullying — and bleeding, he'd grazed the side of his head, his little hands and knees. And Katie was furious. The children called

their parents. I was away at work at the time. And the parents, the *parents*, threatened to call the police if she didn't make him leave. It was awful. These people. Yelling. Calling them both frightful names. Two children. She was upset for months. You can imagine what it did to Gregory. These everyday cruelties were commonplace.

LEYTON-CLARKE. Yet, you know, Julius so often spoke of the emotional pull this country had on him. He would get quite debilitating depressions, from time to time. He made the right choice. For his time and circumstances. The only one. Don't you agree? *(As she looks away, watching her.)* It must have been exciting, being Julius's pupil.

ANNALISE. Oh, heavens … That didn't last long…! I was hopeless, really. Impossibly young. An authentic small town girl. But I loved them. The lessons. And, sometimes, you know, I got something right — it's an indescribably good feeling…!

LEYTON-CLARKE. You know the small pastel I said we'd found? *(She stares at him.)* Posthumously? Among his effects? It's up for sale.

ANNALISE. Up for sale?

LEYTON-CLARKE. *(Nods.)* It's here in our latest catalogue. *(He finds the appropriate page.)*

ANNALISE. But you — Didn't you say it was —

LEYTON-CLARKE. Yes, but we've given it a frame which hides most of the damage. We're not asking much. And it is a van George ["after all"]. *(He holds out the catalogue.)* I thought you might like to see it. *(She takes it. He watches her. The buzzer goes.)* Damn! *(With a grimace.)* Would you excuse me.

ANNALISE. *(Not looking up.)* Oh yes, please do. *(He leaves the room reluctantly. As Annalise gazes at the page, a light comes up on Maraai [in some limbo area of Annalise's mind].)*

MARAAI. *(She holds the box from Scene 1 in her hand.)* … I put the name in here for Miss Anna. Okay? My Abram made the box himself. Miss Anna mustn't worry anymore. Ja, shame, But she mustn't forget us now — up there in Johannesburg. Miss Anna must come and visit us, you hear? Have a good life now, Miss Anna. *(Leyton-Clarke returns, the light on Maraai snaps off.)*

LEYTON-CLARKE. Well, that's taken care of! My assistant will deal with the rest. And we have the night ahead of us!

ANNALISE. I lied, you know.
LEYTON-CLARKE. Oh?
ANNALISE. To my children. About the appraisal. I halved the price.
LEYTON-CLARKE. One hundred and twenty thousand? Sounds good to me. What a pity it isn't for sale.
ANNALISE. Alistair, you wouldn't cheat a harmless old lady *["you're not the type"]*…?!
LEYTON-CLARKE. Certainly I would! I'm willing to *try*. But right now we have a dinner date. And I'm more interested in this secretive nature of yours. You don't confide in anyone?
ANNALISE. *(Deflecting the question.)* I talk to *myself* a lot.
LEYTON-CLARKE. Oh my dear, I recommend it. Does wonders for the soul.
ANNALISE. You don't, do you?
LEYTON-CLARKE. Confide? To all sorts of people!
ANNALISE. No you don't!
LEYTON-CLARKE. Absolutely. Warts 'n all.
ANNALISE. I don't believe a word of it…!
LEYTON-CLARKE. *(Smiles.)* Maybe not. But *you* at least should give it a try.
ANNALISE. I can talk to Kate. As a matter of fact, I intend to.
LEYTON-CLARKE. Good. You can practice with me over dinner.
ANNALISE. I've had my say, Alistair. It's your turn, now. *(Returning the catalogue.)* You can confide in me.
LEYTON-CLARKE. *(Helping her on with her jacket.)* Right. I'll give you a dazzling demonstration. Did you know I knew Julius for almost thirty years? And did I mention his lady? Eileen. Oh yes. Very special. *(They cross to the door.)* And devoted to him. Well, he was an attractive man. Started as his Girl Friday. Became the mainstay of his life. Especially towards the end. I remember, one afternoon, about five winters ago — *(As they exit, Julius van George comes on stage, entering between them. She stops and turns to watch him a moment. Somewhere in this speech, which covers a scene change, Annalise exits unobtrusively.)*
VAN GEORGE. The past? "The past is a foreign country," someone said. *(Beat.)* Once I left, I found out just how deep the roots go. *(Beat.)* But now that I'm back, I discover I've grown new

roots in London! *(Beat.)* I don't belong anywhere now. *(Beat.)* Coming back is like entering a marvelously beautiful madhouse! *(Beat.)* It's too late …

Scene 8

Annalise's living room, in darkness.

We hear Leyton-Clarke and Annalise approaching outside.

LEYTON-CLARKE. *(Coming on stage.)* … you see, for Eileen, the only one who mattered was Julius. And, of course, that suited Julius perfectly.
ANNALISE. That was a delicious dinner, Alistair. Thank you. I haven't had such a good time in years.
LEYTON-CLARK. Then we must do it again.
ANNALISE. I'd like that. Very much.
LEYTON-CLARK. Might I come in?
ANNALISE. Oh, do.
LEYTON-CLARKE. For the briefest moment. Another glimpse of the art treasure.
ANNALISE. Of course. Come in! *(They stare, aghast, as the lights reveal a room that has been ransacked. Contents of cupboards and drawers are emptied on the floor, furniture is overturned, decanters drip liquid onto the carpet …)* No…! Oh my God…! *(She gazes at the blank space on the wall.)* Oh, where's my painting?!
LEYTON-CLARKE. *(Under his breath.)* Good God. *(He bounds forward. From the wreckage beside the desk, he retrieves Annalise's painting. He surveys it, horrified. Part of the canvas seems torn away from the frame, and a large, ugly smear — ice-cream? jam? paint?? — defaces the rest of it.)*
ANNALISE. *(Groans.)* Oh my God…!

End of Act One

ACT TWO

Scene 1

Annalise's living room

The room has been restored to its former condition. The painting, however, is still very much damaged, as can be seen from where it leans propped up in front of the sideboard.

We hear the telephone ring. The answering machine picks up.

ANNALISE'S VOICE. Morant residence. Leave a message please. *(We hear a beep. The lights come up on Imogen, in her limbo area, on the telephone.)*
IMOGEN. Ma, this is awful! Just absolutely awful! And we told you it would happen! Reg told you to let him bar that skylight! We told you to insure it! We even offered to put up half the money, but no, you always know best. And now look what's happened! *(Annalise enters with a shopping bag. She takes off her coat. She sits down and starts to remove the bag's contents [including the following: sketchbook, small boards, paintbrushes, some pastels, tubes of watercolour], savouring the look and feel of everything.)* All because you were so bloody stubborn! I'm sorry, but it's the truth. And now we've lost everything! Honestly, I could scream. It's all bloomingwell gone, because you wouldn't listen! Honestly! I'm sorry, but honestly!!
ANNALISE. "Honestly"...! *(The light on Imogen fades. Annalise continues unpacking her wares. The telephone rings. The answering machine picks up. There's a pause. A beep: The lights come up on Imogen.)*
IMOGEN. *(Contrite.)* Ma, I'm sorry. I didn't mean t — *["to go on like that"]* I apologize. It's just that, it's such a shock. Awful. And

you know that Reg was more than willing to — *["to take care of it all for you"]* I just wish I could *understand*. Why. *(Getting back into her stride.)* For once in your life — just *once*, you couldn't — It was so simple! We'd have taken care of it, and none of this would have happened! *(In full spate again.)* It's the *limit*. The giddy limit! I mean y — *(Realizing she's back where she was in the previous conversation, fighting tears of frustration.)* Oh … Honestly! *(She switches off her phone. The light on Imogen fades.*
ANNALISE. Oh Kate, Katie, when are you coming home…! *(The telephone rings. The answering machine picks up. There's a pause … We hear a beep: The lights come up on Imogen.)*
IMOGEN. Ma, it's me again. Reg says he knows someone in town who can take a look at the painting and give us an ide — *(Staring offstage, alarmed.)* What are you doing, Fiona? No, don't — *Don't* put that — ! Ma, I'll call you back. *(She switches off the phone. The lights on Imogen fade.)*
ANNALISE. Don't call me back…! *(She crosses to her armchair and sinks down into it. She notices the message light flashing on her telephone. Reluctantly, she pushes the button. We hear the electronic voice:)*
ANSWERING MACHINE. You have five messages.
ANNALISE. Oh no…! *(She sighs, pushes the button. A beep:)*
VOICE. *(Bright, very friendly.)* Hello-o…? Ja, this is Joyce. From the "I Spy" Detective Agency…? We've got the information you want. There's quite a lot…! We've even got photographs. I think you'll be very pleased. So, if you'd like to come in and see us, Mrs. Morant, we'll go through all the details with you. Anytime. Okay? Thank you. *(The sound of the receiver going down. Annalise switches off the machine. She sits a moment, lost in thought. Then she gets up, crosses, picks up the painting. About to exit, she turns back to look as the lights come up on:)*

Scene 2

Flashback.

1961. Slade River. The back garden of Julius van George's house.

Another bright, sunny day. The canvas on van George's easel has a large mud splotch right in the center (suggestive of the one on Annalise's damaged painting). As he sets about cleaning it, Young Annalise scolds the (offstage) culprit.

YOUNG ANNALISE. Nigel! That was a terrible thing to do! *(The sound of a small child, crying.)* What made you *do* a thing like that?! Nigel?! Do you *know* what you did?! *(A wail.)* Look at me when I'm talking to you…! I want you to apologize. *(More wailing.)* I want you to come back and say you're sorry. *(Wails and shrieks.)* Do you hear me? Nigel … *(She enters a little way. To van George.)* Is it bad?
VAN GEORGE. *(His manner is a shade more British.)* No, no. The paint was nearly dry …
YOUNG ANNALISE. Thank goodness…! *(To her offstage son.)* Listen to me, Nigel, I want you to think about what you did. And before we leave I want you tell Mr. van George how sorry you are. Okay? *(Nigel off: "Okay … ")* Now stay where Mommy can see you. And behave. Otherwise Lena'll take you straight home. *(Nigel off: "No…! No…!")* All right. *(Crossing back to van George.)* I'm so sorry.
VAN GEORGE. *(Kindly.)* There's no harm done. *(Surveys the canvas with an critical eye.)* It may be an improvement.
YOUNG ANNALISE. *(Remorseful now.)* I shouldn't have yelled like that. I don't know what to do with him. He's become impossible. Every time he doesn't get his way, he — *(Helplessly.)* he does *this* kind of thing.

VAN GEORGE. Well, he's very young.
YOUNG ANNALISE. That's no excuse. Even a four-ye — *especially* a four-year-old, has to learn he can't behave like this! His sister Imogen's much better. *(Watching her offstage son.)* Bossy. But better behaved.
VAN GEORGE. It may be the action of a true art lover. He could grow up to be a critic. They're excellent mud-slingers! *(She watches her son offstage. Van George watches her.)*
YOUNG ANNALISE. Stay where Mommy can see you, Nigel.
LENA. *(Off — calls, in the mid-distance.)* I'll look after him, Miss Anna!
YOUNG ANNALISE. *(Calls.)* Thank you, Lena…! *(It's her turn to watch van George.) Throughout, the air is charged with things unspoken.)* … How long have you been back?
VAN GEORGE. Another interview?
YOUNG ANNALISE. Oh, good heavens!
VAN GEORGE. *(He looks at her.)* A long time ago. *(Turning back.)* It was a clever article.
YOUNG ANNALISE. Too bad they wouldn't print it! But then the Cape *Times* paid me five times more money for it, and everyone here read it anyway. My brief glimpse of fame!
VAN GEORGE. Were they ever able to add to their file?
YOUNG ANNALISE. *(Startled.)* What? Who?
VAN GEORGE. The Special Branch.
YOUNG ANNALISE. … What are you *talking* about?
VAN GEORGE. The police. Haven't they got a file on you?
YOUNG ANNALISE. You're joking!
VAN GEORGE. Why not? They open a file if somebody jaywalks!
YOUNG ANNALISE. They haven't got one on me.
VAN GEORGE. *(Curious.)* You're very certain.
YOUNG ANNALISE. Yes. I am. *(He pulls a cloth over the canvas and focuses on cleaning his brushes.)*
VAN GEORGE. Well, getting married may be the best thing you did.
YOUNG ANNALISE. Why's that?
VAN GEORGE. Mothers don't make good activists. There's too much to lose.
YOUNG ANNALISE. There's too much to *do*!

VAN GEORGE. Your husband, what's his name?
YOUNG ANNALISE. Basil. Morant.
VAN GEORGE. Basil.
YOUNG ANNALISE. I never thought I'd end up in Johannesburg!
VAN GEORGE. "The life of every man is a diary in which he means to write one story, and writes another."
YOUNG ANNALISE. And who said that?
VAN GEORGE. The man who wrote *Peter Pan*!
YOUNG ANNALISE. *(Beat, lightly.)* So, did you miss us? Are you sorry you left?
VAN GEORGE. How did you like Macmillan's speech? *(She looks blank.)* To Parliament.
YOUNG ANNALISE. "The wind of change, blowing through Africa"…?
VAN GEORGE. It got down here — and it blew in the opposite direction!
YOUNG ANNALISE. Well, but there's a lot going on. Ghana's independent now. Kenya —
VAN GEORGE. Kenya…!
YOUNG ANNALISE. — Algeria. And look at America. I like their new president. Kennedy. I'm glad it's not the other one. No, it won't be long now. You'll see. Then you can come back.
VAN GEORGE. It's too late.
YOUNG ANNALISE. *(Lightly.)* It's never too late.
VAN GEORGE. *(Sharply.)* It's often too late.
YOUNG ANNALISE. You're different you know.
VAN GEORGE. "Uppity."
YOUNG ANNALISE. Different.
VAN GEORGE. I share restaurants with whites. Use their bathrooms. *Life* is different.
YOUNG ANNALISE. … I should be going. *(She starts folding a blanket, packing up a few stray toys.)*
VAN GEORGE. I have an exhibition. In London. The Langford Gallery. In April.
YOUNG ANNALISE. That's wonderful.
VAN GEORGE. Your painting. Lend it to me. For the exhibition. *(Seeing her uncertainty.)* It won't cost you anything. They'll collect and return it, door to door. *(Beat.)* We'll look after it, I

promise. *(Beat.)* I won't steal it…!
YOUNG ANNALISE. *(Embarrassed by her transparent reluctance.)* No, no, of course I'll lend it…!
VAN GEORGE. Thank you.
YOUNG ANNALISE. How long will it last? That sounds terrible. You can have it as long as you like. It's just, I'm so used to having it around. It's a part of my life. *(Falters.)* ["I mean"] With the children 'n' things. *(With a laugh.)* Keeps me sane.
VAN GEORGE. I'll get it back safely.
YOUNG ANNALISE. Of course.
VAN GEORGE. It's one of the best I've ever done!
YOUNG ANNALISE. "Even though I say so myself!"
VAN GEORGE. One makes up for the mud-slingers the way one can.
YOUNG ANNALISE. You haven't married yet?
VAN GEORGE. As someone said: "If you cannot be free. Be as free as you can."
YOUNG ANNALISE. *(An edge to her voice.)* You like quotations, don't you.
VAN GEORGE. When I was ten we lived with my Grannie for a year. She had just two books. The *Bible* in High Dutch. And a book of quotations.
YOUNG ANNALISE. Don't you want children?
VAN GEORGE. "As free as you can."
YOUNG ANNALISE. … I have to get back.
VAN GEORGE. Who told you I was here?
YOUNG ANNALISE. Maraai. Our old maid. She's an amazing source of information. You're right, life is complicated for young mothers. I've got to get back to Johannesburg, soon. I'm sure Imogen's daddy's spoiling her rotten. *(Pause.)* … Anyhow, I just came to say hello. *(Pause. She points.)* Do you mind if I look?
VAN GEORGE. … *(Stepping aside.)* Please. *(She crosses, lifts the cloth and looks down at the canvas. He comes to stand beside her.)*
YOUNG ANNALISE. It's — *(She gazes in sad admiration.)* It's very good ["It's exceptional!"].
VAN GEORGE. Do you still paint?
YOUNG ANNALISE. *(Laughs, embarrassed.)* I do. A little. *(Shyly.)* I'm trying watercolours. *(She looks back at the painting.)* This is

marvellous. You can't get light like that with watercolours, can you.
VAN GEORGE. *(Kindly.)* It depends.
YOUNG ANNALISE. *(Getting his meaning.)* Yes, well, not if you're me.
VAN GEORGE. The paper will give you the highlights.
YOUNG ANNALISE. *["Aha!"]* ... Oh! Right!
VAN GEORGE. What happened to pastels? *(For some reason it's a charged moment.)*
YOUNG ANNALISE. It's too hard to fix when you make a mistake. I thought I'd change. *(Beat.)* I have to go. *(As she walks away:)*
VAN GEORGE. Can I get you some roses? For your mother? Legally speaking, they're no longer mine. But what's a legality among friends?
YOUNG ANNALISE. *(Beat, she calls out.)* Nigel — ? Nigel, Mommy's going to pick some roses for Grandma. Okay? I won't be long. And then we're going home. Okay? *(We hear Nigel's four-year-old voice some distance away, chanting: "Okay ... Okay, Mummy, ok — " Then a crash. A shriek. And a huge wail. "Mommy...!" "Mommy...!" "Mommy...!" Calls:)* What? What is it, Nigel?
NIGEL'S VOICE. *(Wildly sobbing:)* I fell ...
YOUNG ANNALISE. What...?
NIGEL'S VOICE. I fell...! *(Young Annalise stares at van George.)* Mommy...!
YOUNG ANNALISE. I'm coming, Nigel. Mommy's coming ...

Scene 4

The same. Some days later.

Leyton-Clarke crosses the room carrying a painting draped with a cloth. He hangs it then steps back as Annalise enters with two glasses of wine.

LEYTON-CLARKE. Ready?
ANNALISE. Yes.
LEYTON-CLARKE. *(Whipping off the cloth.)* There she is…! Right as rain.
ANNALISE. *(Gazing at it with delight.)* Oh Alistair…! *(A little puzzled.)* It looks different. It looks so new…!
LEYTON-CLARKE. It's a good deal cleaner than it used to be. *(Taking his wine.)* I must say, I enjoyed having her. Not sure I want to give her up. *(She looks at him but doesn't answer.)* Well. *(Raising his glass.)* To an absent friend — and his amazing work.
ANNALISE. *(Raising hers.)* And to Alistair Leyton-Clarke!
LEYTON-CLARKE. *(Self-deprecatingly.)* Oh, pooh …
ANNALISE. Does this effect the value now?
LEYTON-CLARKE. … It rather depends. *(Beat.)* You know, it's quite astonishing how little actual damage there was. The chap who restored it said he could have sworn it was done deliberately.
ANNALISE. What?
LEYTON-CLARKE. Minimum harm but for maximum impact.
ANNALISE. … Heavens.
LEYTON-CLARKE. Either that or the most remarkable coincidence. And I'm not sure my chap believes in coincidence.
ANNALISE. *(Becoming aware of a pause she presumably has to fill.)* … Extraordinary.
LEYTON-CLARKE. *(Watching her.)* Any ideas? Annalise? *(She looks at him. Shakes her head.)*
ANNALISE. None. No. Is he sure?

LEYTON-CLARKE. Quite. *(Beat.)* So. It seems that, either way, we were extremely lucky…! *(Afterthought.) You* were.
ANNALISE. *(Distracted.)* Yes. *(Beat, she smiles at him.)* Well. Yet another one of those things that we'll never know — like so much in life. Oh it's wonderful to see her, Alistair. I can't thank you enough.
LEYTON-CLARKE. My great pleasure.
ANNALISE. My children'll be ecstatic. They were terribly upset. Nigel especially … I'm afraid my offspring are in a sorry state. Two of them live beyond their means, and my youngest is in the death throes of a love affair with a married Belgian. And now she's — *(She sips her tea …)* You know *(Beat.)* Nigel spent his stint in the army on the Angolan border. They were the first soldiers there. It was all very clandestine. The Americans were the prime movers … Then they pulled out and left white South Africa to it. The fighting was ferocious. Nigel never spoke about it — well, not to me. One can only imagine … *(Rousing herself.)* But we won't talk about my children! How are you? How's the business?
LEYTON-CLARKE. Going nicely, thank you. Yes … We're making headway with the van Georges we found in Cape Town. They're not bad. Nothing like yours, of course. But they'll pay for the trip with a little over for beer! Oh, *(Fishing in his pockets.)* I thought you'd like to know … *(He brings out a piece of paper.)* Julius wrote something — a quotation — on the back of your "Beauty." *(She looks at him.)* It's by the Irish poet, Thomas Moore. Shall I? *(She nods. He reads:)* "You may break, you may shatter the vase, if you will. But the scent of the roses will hang round it still." *(… He puts the paper on the table.)* Yes … *(Tactfully changing the subject.)* Well, we're finally making progress with this new artist. Mkwayi. Zimbabwean, I think I may have ment —
ANNALISE. *(Over the end of this.)* Alistair, I — *(She stops. He waits. She can't bring herself to speak.)*
LEYTON-CLARKE. Yes?
ANNALISE. … I have something to ask you.
LEYTON-CLARKE. What is it?
ANNALISE. *(Beat.)* I've given it some thought. A great deal of thought.
LEYTON-CLARKE. Yes?

ANNALISE. I'm truly sorry to impose this on you …
LEYTON-CLARKE. I can always say no.
ANNALISE. Well, yes, that's it, you see, it won't be easy, for anyone involved. And from *your* point of view, it can only be a dreadful burden, I realize that.
LEYTON-CLARKE. Isn't that for me to say?
ANNALISE. I've done my best to minimize the aggravation.
LEYTON-CLARKE. Annalise. You're trying to make sure you can swim before you get in the water.
ANNALISE. Well it's rather deep. *(Beat.)* I'm aware that we hardly know each other, Alistair, I'm well aware of that. But I — I really can't think of any — From *my* point of view, there's no one better. Nobody more suitable. In this case. That I'd be comfortable with. Happier. *(Beat.)* We should all do something to redeem our ultimate irrelevance. If we can. Don't you think? Those of us who have become so. *(Nods to herself.)* Yes. But I'll totally understand. I will. If you *[say "no"]* —
LEYTON-CLARKE. Annalise. What is it?
ANNALISE. … First, I want to sell my painting. I'm going to sell her, Alistair. *(She takes his arm.)* On two conditions. *(Leading him U., she begins to tell him …)*

Scene 5

The same. Some days later.

The painting has gone.

The telephone rings. The answering machine picks up.

ANNALISE'S VOICE. Morant residence. Leave a message. *(As the lights come up, Annalise enters with a box and a length of ribbon [which she proceeds to tie around the box, rounding it off with a festive bow]. We hear a beep.)*

FEMALE VOICE. Er — Mrs. Morant, this is … this is Allison at D — Ag! *(Speaking off mike.)* Doctor Goldman, it's the machine.
MALE VOICE. *(Off-mike, in the middle distance — slightly muffled but audible.)* What's that?
FEMALE VOICE. *(Slightly off mike.)* I've got Mrs. Morant's answerphone.
MALE VOICE. *(Off-mike, in the middle distance, but audible.)* Damn! Well, all right, put me through.
ANNALISE. Don't yell at me, Jordan…! *(Sound of a telephone being picked up.)*
MALE VOICE. *(On mike.)* Annalise, Jordan Goldman here. I want you to ring me the moment you get this. Don't be a damn fool. This is not the time to go gallivanting. There's nothing so important that your health doesn't come *first*. Especially now. This is serious, Annalise. *(Annalise places the box inside her already packed suitcase and closes the lid.)* I know you said you need time but, frankly, if we don't deal with this now, you won't have any. And perhaps quite a little more if you *do*! I'm sorry to be brutal … But now I want you in here as soon as possible. Tomorrow. Dammit. *(Beat.)* Dammit. *(Sound of phone being slammed down.)*
ANNALISE. "Dammit." *(To the machine.)* What are my options, Jordan? I get butchered, burned or poisoned…! *(She crosses to her desk and picks up a thick letter already stamped and addressed. After the briefest of pauses, she licks the envelope and presses it down, decisively. She stuffs it into the pouch of her bag.)* Oh, Kate, Katie, I wish I could see your face when you read this. *(She picks up her suitcase. As she starts to leave. Then stops. Sighs.)* One more time…! *(She puts down the suitcase, crosses to the telephone, dials. Disappointed, she waits …)* This is your mother, Nigel. This is the umpteenth message I've left. Where are you? Imogen says you're all okay, so I'm — *(Annalise stops, astonished as Imogen enters. Imogen waves, crosses to sit.)* I'm not going to worry. I expect you know I'm going to Slade River for a few days. I'll be at the Crown Hotel *["Call me!"]*. Well. That's all, then. Just rang to say goodbye. *(Beat.)* And to let you know. *(Beat.)* Love to Christine. Big hug to Ruthie. *(Aware of her daughter, she's about to put the phone down but hesitates then brings it back up to her ear.)* Nigel…? I love you, Nigel. *(She replaces the receiver.)* Imogen.

IMOGEN. Are you ready?
ANNALISE. What are you doing here?
IMOGEN. I'm taking you to the airport.
ANNALISE. But I — No, darling, I —
IMOGEN. *(Over this.)* I *told* you I was.
ANNALISE. I don't nee— *["need you to do that"]*
IMOGEN. *(Picking up Annalise's suitcase.)* You can't go on the bus, Ma, that's absurd.
ANNALISE. Imogen, I'm quite capa — *["capable of going by myself"]*
IMOGEN. I'm not discussing it, come on.
ANNALISE. I thought we'd — *["settled this"]* Really, I don't —
IMOGEN. *(Plonks the suitcase down again.)* Why do you never want me to do anything for you?! You don't. Ever. Never.
ANNALISE. It's not that, I ju —
IMOGEN. If it was Kate *(Indicates the telephone.)* or Nigel, "I love you, Nigel," you'd be happy to go.

ANNALISE.	IMOGEN.
Darling, I — It's just you're very busy. You have … responsibilities. The children.	That's not it. That's not the reason at all, and you know that.

IMOGEN. Oh, forget it. *(She walks away.)* Just forget it…! *(Annalise hurries after her.)*
ANNALISE. No. No. Imogen. Darling. Please, I — I'd like you to take me. I would. *(She hugs her daughter.)* I would. Really. Thank you.
IMOGEN. Well. *(Picking up the suitcase.)* Come along then. We'll have to hurry. The traffic's going to be dreadful. *(Leading the way.)* You know, Fiona's really upset her Grannie's not coming to the game reserve instead. *(The lights fade.)* School holidays are the only time she gets to see you …

Scene 6

The poorer section of Slade River. The next day.

A much older Maraai, sits sunning herself on a small bench, watching the passersby.

Annalise enters, slowly, taking in the scene. She sees the older woman, goes towards her. Maraai looks up, nods politely.

MARAAI. Môre, Mies. *["Good Morning."]* (*She looks away.*)
ANNALISE. Maraai … It's Annalise, Maraai. Annalise Wynand.
MARAAI. … Aaag, my Hete!! *[Oh my lord!]* Miss Anna!!
ANNALISE. … May I sit with you?
MARAAI. Ja-a! Miss Anna can sit! *["that goes without saying"]* (*Annalise sits. The two women look at each other.*)
ANNALISE. … How have you been, Maraai?
MARAAI. Nee, Miss Anna, I've been okay. O-o-ld … I'm very old.
ANNALISE. (*Ruefully.*) We're all old.
MARAAI. What's Miss Anna doing here??
ANNALISE. I came to see you.
MARAAI. Oooh … (*Nodding "I see."*) Why, Miss Anna? *["what are you up to, this time?"]*
ANNALISE. I brought this for you. (*She hands her the gift-wrapped package.*)
MARAAI. (*A formula phrase.*) Haai, Miss Anna mustn't spend her money like that. (*As Annalise opens it for her.*) Ag, is it really you?
ANNALISE. It's been a long time.
MARAAI. Ja … Oooh, a lot of things has happened, nê? *["haven't they."]*
ANNALISE. Things have certainly changed.
MARAAI. Ooh, Miss Anna! I never thought I'd live to see this! Never! Ja, things is different now. (*Dismissively.*) But, ag wat *["nevertheless"]*, they're still the same…!

ANNALISE. *(Lifting out a travelling rug.)* Do you like it? *(She drapes it across Maraai's knees.)*
MARAAI. Oooh …
ANNALISE. So you have been okay?
MARAAI. Ja wat. *[dismissively: "yeah, sure"]* With the pension your Ma gave me and the money Miss Anna sent, we didn't do too bad. *(Confidentially.)* When I left Mrs. Hof, she gave me just *ten little rands!* Imagine! Ten! Gah! *["disgusting isn't it"]* It's good to see Miss Anna again — how's Miss Anna's family?
ANNALISE. All gone. Grown up and gone.
MARAAI. *(Cheerfully.)* Ja, mine too! Even my Hansie. He was a fisherman, like his father but, ag, there's no more fish in the sea! So he went to Cape Town. He's getting married. At last. December 2nd. *(With satisfaction.)* They're all gone! *["at last!"]* It's so nice *["finally!"]* just to sit here in the sun. Doing nothing.
ANNALISE. And there's the Sleeping Beauty.
MARAAI. *(Cheerfully.)* Ja wat, she's still there.
ANNALISE. *(Gazing at it.)* Lovely …
MARAAI. *(Mildly, matter of factly.)* Is Miss Anna sick?
ANNALISE. I'm not too well, Maraai.
MARAAI. *(Sighs.)* Ja…! *(She gives a helpless little chuckle: "welcome to the club.")* My old *bones* is so sore … Aag…! I never thought I'd see Miss Anna, *ever* again. *(Patting Annalise's knee in emphasis.)* And here you are. *(Annalise smiles at her.)*
ANNALISE. You were my friend. My good, good friend. *(Beat.)* Do you remember you helped me once? You did me a big favor, Maraai.
MARAAI. *(Nodding.)* Ja-a. I remember — ooh — but that was a *long* time ago. *(Annalise produces a small collection of papers.)* What's this?
ANNALISE. *(Handing her a single sheet.)* A marriage document. Look at the name. *(Maraai studies it. She gasps in astonishment.)*
MARAAI. Haai, *["goodness"]* Miss Anna…??
ANNALISE. Is that her?
MARAAI. *(Nods.)* Allamapstieks!! *[goodness gracious!]* How did Miss Anna get this??
ANNALISE. A detective agency. *(Handing her some photographs.)* And look at these. *(Maraai scrutinizes them.)*

MARAAI. Ooh, Miss Anna…? Is this her? And these are the children, nê? *(Annalise nods.)* Look, little twins! *(Hands them all back.)* What's all this for? *(She looks at Annalise with some of her old suspicion ["a leopard doesn't change its spots"])* Hê? What's Miss Anna going to do?
ANNALISE. I want you to help me again, Maraai. It's very important. I need you to do me one last favor. *(Maraai stares at her … The lights fade.)*

Scene 7

Flashback.

Slade River. October 1951. The rose park at Slade River. Two days later.

Annalise enters slowly. She gazes around remembering the house, the topography no longer there.

She crosses to a park bench, sits down and proceeds to take out her old box of pastels (the same one van George hands her in Act One, Scene 2). She opens it, places it next to her then takes up her sketch book. But as she starts to draw, the memories take over … (the following scene takes place around her).

Julius van George enters the rose garden. A barefoot Young Annalise follows. She has her sketchbook in hand, and he, a basket of roses and a pair of sécateurs. They're laughing.

YOUNG ANNALISE. … And did you see the headline in this morning's paper?
VAN GEORGE. No.
YOUNG ANNALISE. About the mining accident? I can't believe anyone wrote something so stupid. It says: "Groaning Man Could Be *Alive*." *(He laughs.)* And there's an article, just as bizarre. In a dif-

ferent way. The Pretoria Women's Agricultural Union says that milk from the cows of non-white farmers can't be mixed with the milk from white farmers' cows. I *mean!* Honestly! Aren't you going to miss us? This country.

VAN GEORGE. Lena told me Mr. Prinsloo beat Pieter Jonkers half to death the other day. And shot and killed his dog.

YOUNG ANNALISE. ... *Why?*

VAN GEORGE. It got into their yard and mated with his wife's part pedigree poodle.

YOUNG ANNALISE. Oh God.

VAN GEORGE. He says he'll drown the puppies when they come.

YOUNG ANNALISE. Why did you tell me that?

VAN GEORGE. It's why I won't miss this country. Why I'm going.

YOUNG ANNALISE. That's a lie! That's not why. Don't lie.

VAN GEORGE. *(Over the end of this.)* No. It's why I'm *glad* to go...!

YOUNG ANNALISE. Running away. You don't care what happens here.

VAN GEORGE. What do you think I should do about it?

YOUNG ANNALISE. Fight. Stay and fight.

VAN GEORGE. And how should I fight? Tell me. They're taking us off the voters' role. Should I petition the four white straw men they say will represent us?

YOUNG ANNALISE. But don't you care about us? Your country?

VAN GEORGE. I'm a painter, Annalise! *That's* my life! That's how I speak. I paint! I'm *good!* Exceptional! And not good for anything else. I just paint.

YOUNG ANNALISE. What about this defiance campaign? *(He stares at her.)* In Johannesburg. I read about it. Look at that!

VAN GEORGE. *(Laughs.)* How naïve you are ...

YOUNG ANNALISE. Oh yes? Well, if I'm naïve there's a lot of other naïve people around. Pretty clever and accomplished naïve people.

VAN GEORGE. And all of them are going to jail. It's not going to get better.

YOUNG ANNALISE. Not if you don't fight.

VAN GEORGE. *You* fight. It's your bloody government! *(Silence. She crosses to the bench and sits down [next to her older self]. She picks out a pastel from the box and starts to draw. He looks at her ...)* I'll

come back. You'll see. One day, they'll *invite* me back! *(Silence.)*
YOUNG ANNALISE. ... So, anyway. *[a quasi ritual]* Here's a joke. Do you want to hear it?
VAN GEORGE. Tell me.
YOUNG ANNALISE. *(Jollying herself up as she goes along.)* Okay. Van der Merwe has a new job as a bus conductor, and his liberal boss from England is coming to visit. Of course he wants to impress his boss, so he takes him down to the bus terminal. All the passengers are waiting. Van der Merwe says to them: "Now listen, before I let youse all on the bus I want to tell you, straightaway, *I don't have any color prejudice.* So far as I'm concerned, you could all be *blue!* Okay? Good! Now, you can get on the bus — pale blues in the front, dark blues at the back." *(They laugh.)* You'll be sorry! They don't have van der Merwe where you're going.
VAN GEORGE. I hope not!
YOUNG ANNALISE. You'll miss some things.
VAN GEORGE. I'll miss a lot. *(They stare at each other.)*
YOUNG ANNALISE. ... I need some more roses. *(He holds out the sécateurs but, as she takes them for a brief moment he doesn't relinquish them, so that she's held there, facing him. He watches her cross to the rose bushes.)*
VAN GEORGE. I've finished your painting. *(She stops. She turns to him.)*
YOUNG ANNALISE. ... Thank you.
VAN GEORGE. It's good. It's brilliant. One of the best I've ever done.
YOUNG ANNALISE. Do you have to go?
VAN GEORGE. *(Over the end of this.)* More than ever! Now more than ever. *(She turns away. She is just visible now, amongst the rose bushes. And van George, Annalise and her younger self are in a direct diagonal as he says:)*
VAN GEORGE. And you, Annalise? What will you do? *(Young Annalise concentrates on the roses ...)* Will you go back to college? *(Pause.)* I love your jokes! Do you have any more? *(He crosses toward her, coming to a stop at the park bench, next to the older Annalise.)* To help me through the grey days? Remind me what I've left behind. *(As he gazes down, introspectively, it seems as though he's looking directly at the older woman.)*

YOUNG ANNALISE. *(Emerging from behind the rose bushes.)* Uh … Ja…! *(Doing her best.)* … Ja, I — I've got a couple more. Um … Okay. *(Beat.)* So! Van der Merwe's helping at the church bazaar. He's going to be the fortune teller. So they brief him beforehand, and they say: "Listen van der Merwe, you can say what you like but for God's sake be tactful." So, his first customer comes in … And van der Merwe looks at the man's palm … and — *(She points. He grins, holds out his hand. She approaches. Without touching it, she bends over the palm and peers at it.)* And he says: "Jerrr, man, the next ten years are going to be terrible!" His customer panics. "An — and after that?" he asks. And van der Merwe says: "No man, after that, you'll get used to it!" *(He laughs. She joins in.)*
YOUNG ANNALISE. You'll get used to it. *(The laughter dies into silence and, close now, they gaze at each other.)* I thought … Maybe, you know, perhaps I'd go overseas ["as well"]. *(We, like she, can see his rejection of this offer as he backs away ever so slightly, shifting his glance. Recovering her pride.)* But I think I'll get my diploma first. *(Struggling with her humiliation, the anger and the hurt, she sets about collecting her things [she puts down his sécateurs, crosses to pick up her sketchbook].)* Ja. Probably. "Something to fall back on," as my mother says.
VAN GEORGE. *(Over the end of this.)* She's right.
YOUNG ANNALISE. Ja! Well I hope whoever gets the house, looks after your roses.
VAN GEORGE. *(Over the end of this.)* My brother'll move in.
YOUNG ANNALISE. *(Over the end of this.)* Good. *(She crosses down to the rose basket, dumps the book in it.)*
VAN GEORGE. *(Over this.)* Till it's settled.
YOUNG ANNALISE. *(Crossing U. with the basket. Over this.)* Good. That's good. *(She drops the basket on the ground, marches D. again. Fighting her tears.)* So here's your other joke…! They were going to put on "The Marriage of Figaro." *(Losing the battle.)* … At the church hall. So they send van der Merwe an invita — *(He crosses to her swiftly. She turns with a sob as he grabs her in his arms. All the underlying sexual tension that was there throughout the scene gives way as, finally, they kiss … They break. They kiss again. With greater urgency. As they break this time, and aware of the danger, with their arms around each other they exit quickly. The lights go to black.)*

Scene 8

The Rose Park.

A tight spot lights Annalise's face. As she speaks, the light gradually spreads to show the rest of her where she sits on the bench, then to illuminate the roses, the mountains behind her — and, just discernably, the outline of a figure at the other end of the bench. Finally, the lights fully reveal the other woman — a light skinned Coloured woman in her late forties/early fifties — clearly.

ANNALISE. I want to tell you our story. In the beginning. When we shared a story ... *(Beat.)* When I knew that you were there, I was deathly afraid. What I had done, what had happened, was a crime. An immoral act. It said so in the statute books. And we would go to jail. That was the law, back in the fifties. *(Beat.)* So scared ... For you would be the living proof that I had done this deed. And was a criminal. White woman who'd loved a man who wasn't. Who never knew he'd fathered you. Your warm and cinnamon colored skin, soft and smooth as rose petals. As you lay asleep in my arms. So beautiful. Perdita. My lost one. First child. The one I gave away. *(By now the lights have revealed Annalise's tiny corner of the park, it spreads in slow stages to the larger area behind her during the following.)* He had gone. Your father. I was alone with this big, big secret. And what to do? If they knew, it would ruin my parents. My mother would die for the shame of it. I had to get rid of these cells inside me. That, too, was against the law. Officially the lesser crime. They couldn't judge a thimbleful of cells. But where to go? A squalid back street? I didn't know another way. Some horrid stranger. ... Destroying you? I couldn't. Couldn't do that. And all this while you were there inside me: changing, unfolding, becoming you. Bound and determined. You and my body in special partnership. According to some infinitely greater laws. So I did the only thing I could. I left my world and entered the one that would one day be yours. Astonishing how easily I could navigate, how quickly the connections formed. In that world. Where this was just an everyday catastrophe. Where details and documents were a haphazard affair. Back there, three women only shared my secret. *(Wonders at it.)* And kept it ... *(Orienting herself somewhat toward the other end of the bench.)* And so I left Slade River. I went back to the College. Found a room in a boarding house, went to lectures, to the library, went shopping, did my laundry, tried to concentrate. Hid your growing presence under shapeless clothes ... The days had no validity...! *(The light is spreading further. Enough to give the outline of the other presence.)* And in the dark and sleepless nights I tried to tell you everything. Enough to last a lifetime. And made my hopeless plans to keep you. The more impossible they were, the more obsessive they became. And how I hated the men who'd made those laws. Made our act of love a crime so reprehensible. With all my heart I hated them. And how I loved you. My overwhelming secret. Lying, curled inside me, listening. My only friend. My child I would betray. And remember till I draw my last breath. *(The lights begin revealing the other woman clearly now.)* Then winter came. And in an outlaw nursing home, you arrived. What should have been a wondrous thing. A joyous celebration. Was full of shame and grief ... *(Beat.)* I knew you'd be a little girl. I held you. Kept you so close to me. Until they came. They took you away. I ga — *["gave you away"]* I gave — ... *(Pause.)* Then I slipped back into my world. Took up my life again. "New chapter." "Don't look back." "Try and forget." "Best to put it all behind you." And there were babies, babies ... Babies everywhere. But I never saw your face again. You were growing up. Going to school. Turning into someone else. Calling somebody else your mother. I hope she was kind. Please say that she was kind. *(The woman smiles faintly.)* You had gone for good. But you never left me. I would watch my other children play and see you there. My shadow child. A little taller, little darker. My lost one. *(Beat.)* Serena. That's a pretty name. Serena. *(Beat.)* I never tried to seek you out. I'm not your mother. I gave that right away. We're strangers now. But I have to tell you how I loved you; what the pain was, losing you; how I've thought of you and thought of you;

that your shadow never leaves ... *(Beat.)* I want to tell you who your father was. Julius. He was an artist. Julius van George. His house was here. These were his roses ... He never knew. He'd gone, you see, he'd left. He never knew. He never had another child. Just you. Serena ... It's a pretty name. *(The lights go to black. In the scene change, the lights come up on Kate [in a limbo space] on her cell phone.)*

KATE. Hello, Crown Hotel? Yes, Mrs. Morant please ... Well, I'd like to leave a voice mail ... Mommy, it's me! I'm home! Sooner than I thought. I heard your message — very mysterious. And I've got the letter you say is going to "explain everything" — it's right here in my hot little hand — but, *first* I have to tell you, Jean-Pierre and I are back together! I know what you're going to say but it's what I want. Dunno how long it'll last ... But, what the hell...! *(Beat.)* But the better news is: I'm flying down to Slade River! I'll be there for dinner. *(Opening the envelope of Annalise's letter ...)* Can't wait to be with you. We'll have a great time! So, that's my news...! Now, about your phone message, yes, I'll certainly give Leyton-Clarke a call ... *(Withdrawing the letter, she looks at the five tightly hand-written pages with astonishment and concern.)* ... though I'm not quite sure what for ... *(Her eyes glance over the first page ...)* Tell you what ... Why don't I read the letter, and I'll call you right back. 'Bye. *(She turns her phone off and starts to read ... The lights go to black.)*

Scene 9

Four months later. The Johannesburg office of an overseas firm of art dealers.

Leyton-Clarke stands facing Annalise's three children (who occupy three of the four chairs in the room) each holding a copy of her will. (Leyton-Clarke has noticeably more pages than they do.)

For Kate, the following is not new territory and her reactions reflect that.

LEYTON-CLARKE. It's quite simple. As you see, apart from any outstanding debts, taxes, stamp duties and the like (and, of course, funeral expenses) the rest of your mother's estate (there's not a great deal but what there is) is divided equally among the three of you. And … *(Sorting through his papers.)* Ah yes. Your mother also stipulates that anyone contesting any part of her will, will forfeit his or her share unconditionally. *(Smiles.)* I'm sure that won't occur.
NIGEL. There's nothing here about the painting. What about the painting?
IMOGEN. Yes.
LEYTON-CLARKE. Ah, yes. The painting. Excuse me a moment. *(He buzzes an intercom.)* Jacqueline, have we heard from Mrs. Claasens yet? Jacqueline *(A voice Through the intercom.)* Not yet, Mr. Leyton-Clarke.
LEYTON-CLARKE. Well, buzz me as soon as she arrives, will you? Jacqueline. *(A voice Through the intercom.)* Of course. *(He returns to the children. He looks round at them. Smiles.)*
LEYTON-CLARKE. Well now, as you know, the formal reading of a will isn't, of course, necessary. But it was your mother's express wish that there be one. With all the adult beneficiaries present. But also, that it *not* be done until certain conditions were satisfied.

And, that the will's contents not be divulged until such time. *(He smiles at Nigel.)* In response to Mr. Morant's enquiry, I mailed you each a copy of your mother's letter to me where she emphasizes this most emphatically. I would have done so sooner but I was in the Far East when I got the news. In point of fact, your mother's death was somewhat unexpected. We all knew she had cancer, *(He looks at her children, who shift uncomfortably.)* of course. But no one suspected the embolism.

IMOGEN. Mr. Leyton-Clarke, I don't want to be rude but will we be here much longer? If my mother's will is so simple … I mean, is there a problem…? With the painting?

LEYTON-CLARKE. No. No problem.

IMOGEN. In that case … *(She looks at him enquiringly: "what's the holdup?")*

LEYTON-CLARKE. *(Checking his watch.)* I think we can go ahead. There was to be one other adult present, but …

IMOGEN. A beneficiary?

LEYTON-CLARKE. Yes.

IMOGEN. A beneficiary??

LEYTON-CLARKE. Yes. But I'm sure we can proceed. There are two codicils to your mother's will. One appointing me her executor. And a second and separate one — which I have here — dealing with her wishes regarding the painting. I'm pleased to say that in the space of these four months we were able to sell it, as per your mother's wishes, for a substantial sum of money. *(Nigel takes out a pocket calculator.)* The net proceeds after expenses, commission et cetera amount to — and, as the sale was made in London, I have left the amount in sterling. *(Searching for them.)* Yes, here we are. "Three hundred and fifteen thousand, two hundred and forty-six pounds *(To Nigel, who's busily punching keys.)* — and eighty-two pence." And, as you know, the conversion to South African rands is extremely favorable — more than ten times the amount. *(The intercom buzzes. Leyton-Clarke crosses to it.)* Yes?

JACQUELINE. *(A voice Through the intercom.)* You asked me to buzz you, Mr. Leyton-Clarke, when Mrs. Claasens arrived, well she's just called to say she's on her way. Did you want to speak with her?

LEYTON-CLARKE. Yes. Thank you. I'll be right out. *(To the children.)* Would you excuse me for a moment. *(He exits.)*

NIGEL. Three million, four hundred thousand rand...! Jesus. *(He and Imogen grin at each other — he gives her a jubilant peck on the cheek. Kate looks on, non-committal.)* Not bad, hey...?!
IMOGEN. *(Triumphant.)* Reg *thought* it would be more than Ma said...!
NIGEL. It's spectacular...! *(Noticing Kate, uncomfortable.)* Oh come on, Kate...! Admit it. You get a share, you know.
KATE. Did I say anything?
IMOGEN. It was Mom's wish. In the end. To sell it. *(To Nigel, who nods.)* And I mean what else? *["what else could we have done with it?"]*
NIGEL. Right. *(He looks back at his younger sister, sensing something judgemental.)* Aaah, Kate...!
KATE. Did I say something, Nigel?
NIGEL. You didn't *need* to …
IMOGEN. *(Teary.)* Poor Ma. *(Blowing her nose.)* I miss her you know...!
NIGEL. Of course. We all do.
IMOGEN. *(Watching his younger sister closely.)* He's right, though, Kate. You've haven't said a word the whole time. You were the last to see Ma. Did she — I dunno … Did she ev —
KATE. Why don't we hear Leyton-Clarke out.
IMOGEN. *(To Nigel.)* What about this other beneficiary...?? Ma never m — *["never mentioned anyone of that name, ever."]* *(Leyton-Clarke reenters.)*
LEYTON-CLARKE. *(He's quietly relishing this.)* Mrs. Claasens is still en route. But, I have her permission to proceed without her. So. Where were we? Ah, yes, the painting. There was one further deduction. *(Nigel's calculator is at the ready.)* Your mother asked to purchase, from the proceeds of the sale, a small pastel by the same artist, Julius van George.
IMOGEN. *(Perplexed.)* She bought another painting?
LEYTON-CLARKE. She did. That left a total of three hundred and seven thousand, four hundred and five pounds. *(Nigel adjusts his figure.)* Of *that* amount, it was your mother's wish that fifteen percent go to a Slade River Trust Fund set up to preserve the mountainside flora and fauna and for the maintenance of the town's parks. *(Nigel re-calculates.)* The three of you are trustees.

(He waves some papers.) I have all the relevant documentation. A further five per cent — *(Nigel calculates.)* — is to go to *(Reads.)* "a Mrs. Maraai Matthys of 55 Melkhout Laan, Slade River." With a stipulation: *(Reads.)* "In the event that said Maraai Matthys does not survive me or dies within sixty days of my death, I direct that her share revert to my estate." *(Beat.)* I'm sorry to say Mrs. Matthys did die. *(He watches Nigel's furious calculations ...)* But she survived your mother by seventy-one days, so her share belongs to her heirs. *(Nigel gives up.)* Of the *remaining* amount — and this is with a provision for any children Kate will have — *half* is to go to your mother's existing eight grandchildren in equal parts *(Continuing unperturbed over the interruptions.)* to be held in trust for each child until that child turns twen —
IMOGEN. W — Wait. Mr. Leyton-Clarke. Wait.
NIGEL. My mother has only four grandchildren. *(Kate watches but avoids meeting any glances thrown in her direction by her siblings.)*
LEYTON-CLARKE. Ah. Yes, well, in point of fact, she has ei —
IMOGEN. Four. She has four grandchildren, Mr. Leyton-Clarke. My two and Nigel's two. That makes four. Unless Kate's having quads.
LEYTON-CLARKE. *(Beat, referring to the document in hand.)* The remaining half ... is to be shared equally among her four children, with the small pastel going to her eldest *(He drops his bombshell.)* "Mrs. Serena Claasens." With the usual proviso that if any one of her children does not survive her by sixty days etc. etc. ... *(He looks at the stupefied faces.)* ... Any questions? *(Pause.)*
IMOGEN. Who?
LEYTON-CLARKE. Mrs. Claasens. Serena Claasens was your mother's first child, Mrs. Ellis, your half-sister, whom she gave up for adoption. Before she married.
IMOGEN. I don't believe you.
LEYTON-CLARKE. Yes ... Well, we have all the papers here. Plus this affidavit *(He crosses to Imogen.)* signed by your mother ... *(Handing it to her.)* to the effect that *(His second bombshell.)* Mrs. Claasens' natural father was *(He points.)* Julius van George. *(Another, stupefied pause.)*
NIGEL. But he — He's — *(He catches himself. The unstated hangs in the air ...)*

LEYTON-CLARKE. Yes … Quite. *(There's a buzz from the intercom.)* Ah! That'll be Mrs. Claasens, now. *(Answers.)* Yes, Jacqueline?
JACQUELINE. *(A voice through the intercom.)* Mrs. Claasens is here, Mr. Leyton-Clarke.
LEYTON-CLARKE. Yes. Thank you. Send her in. *(The door to Leyton-Clarke's office opens. Serena Claasens enters. Framed in the doorway in the act of entering, her hand still on the knob, she registers the room's occupants — as they do her. The scene freezes. Van George enters D. He runs on, stops, looks around expectantly. Moments later, Young Annalise appears, clutching her sketchbook and pastels. They sit down side by side and, together, they begin to draw, collaborating on the same picture [the little pastel with the "strange rose petal clouds"]. But, in essence, it's less about art than about falling in love as, in that moment, both are purely and simply happy, with life and with each other.)*

The End

The authors of JULIUS VAN GEORGE'S quotations are:

"Art, like morality, consists in drawing the line somewhere."
(G.K. Chesterton, 1874 – 1936)

"The past is a foreign country … "
(L.P. Hartley, 1895 – 1972)

"The life of every man is a diary in which he means to write one story, and writes another."
(J.M. Barrie, 1860 – 1937)

"If you cannot be free. Be as free as you can."
(Ralph Waldo Emerson, 1803 – 1882)

AUTHOR'S NOTE

The jokes in this play are not original material, but, to the best of my knowledge, their sources are untraceable.

ROUGH PRONUNCIATION GUIDE TO AFRIKAANS

The single vowels "a," "e," "o" are pronounced as in Spanish.

The "ê" sound is also like the Spanish.

"e" in a final syllable or following a "t" or "s" is pronounced as a shwa sound — i.o.w. as the "a" in the word "about."

The "i" sound is a shwa sound.

The "aa" is the same sound as "a" *(above)* except longer.

The "ee" sound is pronounced as in the English word "heel" or the English name "Ian."

The "oe" sound is like a Spanish "u."

The "ie" sound is like a Spanish "i."

The "ei" sound is pronounced as in the English word "ate" or "hey."

The "oo" sound is like the sound in the English word "poor."

The "aai" sound is like the sound in the English word "buy."

The "oei" sound is a combination of an English "oo" followed by an English "ee." (a bit like the word "phooeey" or a "dark" version of "chewy" — the "u" is darker).

The "r" is rolled as in Spanish (except Maraai tends *not* to roll them).

The "v" is pronounced as an "f."

The "w" is pronounced as a "v."

The h is a "voiced" sound. (Instead of just using breath to say "h," the larynx comes into play, making the sound heavier or darker — almost as in the expression "huh?")

A "t" is a "t."

A "d" is a "d" except when it's final, when it becomes a "t."

A "k" or "kk" is a "k."

The "j" initially is pronounced as a "y" (as in "yes").

An initial "g" is the "throat-clearing sound" in the Scottish word "loch" or the *Castilian* Spanish "j." Similarly, the final "g" in the word "wag" (and the word "magtig" has two such sounds).

The final "ng" in the word "ding" is as in English "wing," except that in Afrikaans the "i" sound is a flat, shwa sound *(see above)*.

In the word "hete" (on page 37) the first "e" is said as an "ee" would be, and the second "e" is said as a shwa. (So the first part word would sound almost like "yeah.")

PRONUNCIATION OF SESOTHO

As the Sesotho is not meant to be understood by Annalise or the audience, the following pronunciation guide should be sufficient to ensure an adequate level of authenticity:

The stress is usually on the penultimate syllable. As in any language, the short or unstressed words tend to "run together," especially when the language is spoken quickly.

The "h" sound:
— in the word "hau" (page 39), the "h" is voiced [ɦau].
— The "h" sound in combination with another consonant is usually silent, present as a "breath" following the consonant before. Its appearance indicates that the preceding consonant is more accentuated, aspirated, more heavily plosive as the case may be. The "h" on its own is a harder, more voiced sound. "Hall" — hl is pronounced as in Welsh "ll" — [i.e., a guttural German "ch" followed by an "l"].

k, l, m, n, p, r, s, t, w, as in English. Initial m's and n's are voiced (i.e., produced in the larynx).

a	as in "ah"
b	quite plosive — as in "b<u>e</u>lt"
bj	= "bzh"
d	the tongue may be further back than for English
e	between an "ay" and an "ee" sound
ê	"eh" — close to the Spanish sound
f	in English the teeth and bottom lip are used — here only the lips are
fh	see "f" and see note on "h" above
fs	= "fsh"
g	the guttural German "ch"
h	see above
i	as in "it" but slightly elongated
o	close to a "u" — as in the first part of the diphthong "p<u>oo</u>r"
ô	as in Spanish
u	as in "ball<u>oo</u>n"
y	as in "<u>y</u>es"
ng	= "singer"
ny	= Spanish ñ
kg	k + guttural German "ch"
kh	heavily aspirated

ph	"p" aspirated [and *not* as in English]
sw	as in "sweet"
th	= t with aspiration [and *not* as in English]
tl	pronounced as a single sound, as in "butler"
tlh	more aspirated than tl
ts	between "ba<u>ts</u>" and "<u>ch</u>ief"
tsh	more aspirated than ts
s	tends to be more of a "sh"

NOTE ON THE PRONUNCIATION (IN IPA) OF CHARACTER AND PROPER NAMES

ANNALISE	[ˈænəˌliːz] (LEYTON-CLARKE)
	[ˈʌnəˌlis] (JULIUS and ANNALISE)
MARAAI	[məˈrɑi]
MORANT	[mɔˈrænt]
TSHIPI	Between [tsipi] and [tʃipi]
VAN GEORGE	[væn ˈdʒɔːdʒ] [*]
WYNAND	[ˈveinʌnt]

Page 20	Hanepoot [**]	[ˈħanəˌpuət]
Page 24	Lena	[ˈlɪənʌ]
Page 30	Mkwayi	[mˈkuaɿi]
Page 31	Rands [***]	[rændz] (NIGEL)
Page 41	Rand [***]	[rɑnt] (TSHIPI)
Page 46	Abram	[ˈɑːbrʌm]
Page 62	Mrs. Hof	[hɔf]
Page 62	Hansie	[ˈħãsi]
Page 64	Prinsloo	[ˈprənsluə]
Page 64	Pieter Jonkers	[ˈpitər ˈjɔŋkərs]
Page 65	van der Merwe [****]	[ˌfʌn ə ˈmɛrvə]
Page 70	Claasens	[ˈklɑːsəns]
Page 73	Mattys	[mɑˈteɪs]
Page 73	Melkhout Laan	[ˈmelkhout ˌlɑːn]

[*] Pronounced this (the English) way throughout except by Young Annalise in Act One, Scene 2 when she pronounces the van [fʌn].
[**] Derived from "honey pots." The large green muscat grapes of Alexandria.
[***] South African currency (after 1960) used interchangeably in the plural, with or without the "s." And sometimes pronounced differently by the different language groups.
[****] The stereotypical "dumb" white Afrikaner — somewhat endearing in a gruesome kind of way.

AFRIKAANS
Glossary and phonetic [IPA] pronunciation

In some cases pronunciations are given as the word/phrase would sound when said colloquially, in conversation.

ACT ONE
Note: the word "Ja" *(Yes)* [ja] occurs frequently throughout the text.

Scene 2

Page	Word/Phrase	Pronunciation
20	Allamapstieks!	[alʌ ˈmɑpstiks]
20	Nee!	[nɪə]
20	Gah [*]	[xa]
24	Magtig!	[ˈmɑxtəx]
24	Ag	[ax]
24	Dê!	[de]

Note: All of Maraai's Oooh's are [u] and not [ou]

Scene 4

Page	Word/Phrase	Pronunciation
34	Veldt [**] koppies [***]	[felt] [ˈkɔpiz]

Scene 5

Page	Word/Phrase	Pronunciation
37	O hete!	[uə ˈhɪətə]
37	Lekker, lekker [****]	[ˈlekʌ ˈlekʌ]
37	Nê	[ne]
37	Ag, shame [*****] (also "ja, [ja] shame" page 46)	[ax ʃeɪm]

[*] An exclamation of disgust or disgusted surprise.
[**] Savannah.
[***] Hills with rocky outcrops resembling a head.
[****] Literally "nice," but its meaning is often stronger, as in "delicious," "terrific," "great." The double use of the word is common, and it should be said as a single word.
[*****] In South African English, an exclamation of warm sympathy.

ACT TWO

Scene 6

Page	Word/Phrase	Pronunciation
61	Môre Mies	[ˈmɔrə ˌmis]
61	Aaag, My Hete	[aːːx] *(simply a long drawn-out "Ag")* [meɪ ˈħɪətə]
61	Haai	[ħɑɪ]
61	Nê	[ne]
61	Ag wat	[ˈɑːx vɑt]
63	Hê?	[ħe]

Scene 7

Page	Word/Phrase	Pronunciation
66	Jerrr [*]	[jɪər:::]

[*] A corruption of the word "Here" (Lord).

PROPERTY LIST

Brandy decanter and glasses
Easel, canvas, and paints, old radio, basket of vegetables
Wine in carafe, glasses, crudites, napkins
Canvas painting, cloth, oil painting brushes
Radio
Four copies of a last will and testament (extra copies for LEYTON-CLARKE: codicil #2, trusteeship documents, affidavit)
Cup and teapot (ANNALISE)
Box with old photos and papers (IMOGEN, ANNALISE, MARAAI)
"Same" box, filled with pastels (VAN GEORGE, ANNALISE, YOUNG ANNALISE)
Milktart (ANNALISE)
Box camera, notebook and pencil (YOUNG ANNALISE)
Basket of roses (VAN GEORGE)
Rose cutters (VAN GEORGE)
Basket of grapes, 4 shillings (MARAAI)
Painting (LEYTON-CLARKE)
Damaged painting (ANNALISE)
Cell phone (LEYTON-CLARKE)
Hurricane lamp, easel, crate (ANNALISE)
Blue paper in the box (ANNALISE)
Gun (ANNALISE)
Money, 200-plus Rand (ANNALISE)
Pills (ANNALISE)
Catalogue (ANNALISE)
Art supplies in shopping bag (ANNALISE)
Blanket and toys (ANNALISE)
2 wine glasses (ANNALISE)
Box and ribbon, suitcase (ANNALISE)
Thick letter (ANNALISE, KATE)
Gift-wrapped box containing a lap rug (ANNALISE)
Document, photos (ANNALISE)
Sketchbook (ANNALISE, YOUNG ANNALISE)
Business card (LEYTON-CLARKE)
Telephone book (Yellow Pages) (ANNALISE)
Slip of paper with quotation (LEYTON-CLARKE)
Cell phone (KATE)
Pocket calculator (NIGEL)

SOUND EFFECTS

Car hooter
Car doors closing, car starting
V/O, Radio
Phone ring, answered by machine beeping
Phone machine message
V/O, Annalise
V/O, Lena
V/O, phone message, Allison, Dr. Goldman
V/O, phone message, Joyce
V/O, Voices 1, 2, 3
Doorbell
Buzzer
V/O, intercom, Jacqueline

AUTHOR'S NOTE

In addition to the opening, intermission and closing music, several bars of original music were composed as punctuation to scenes and to cover scene changes, including a beautiful, haunting refrain heralding the first flashback scene.

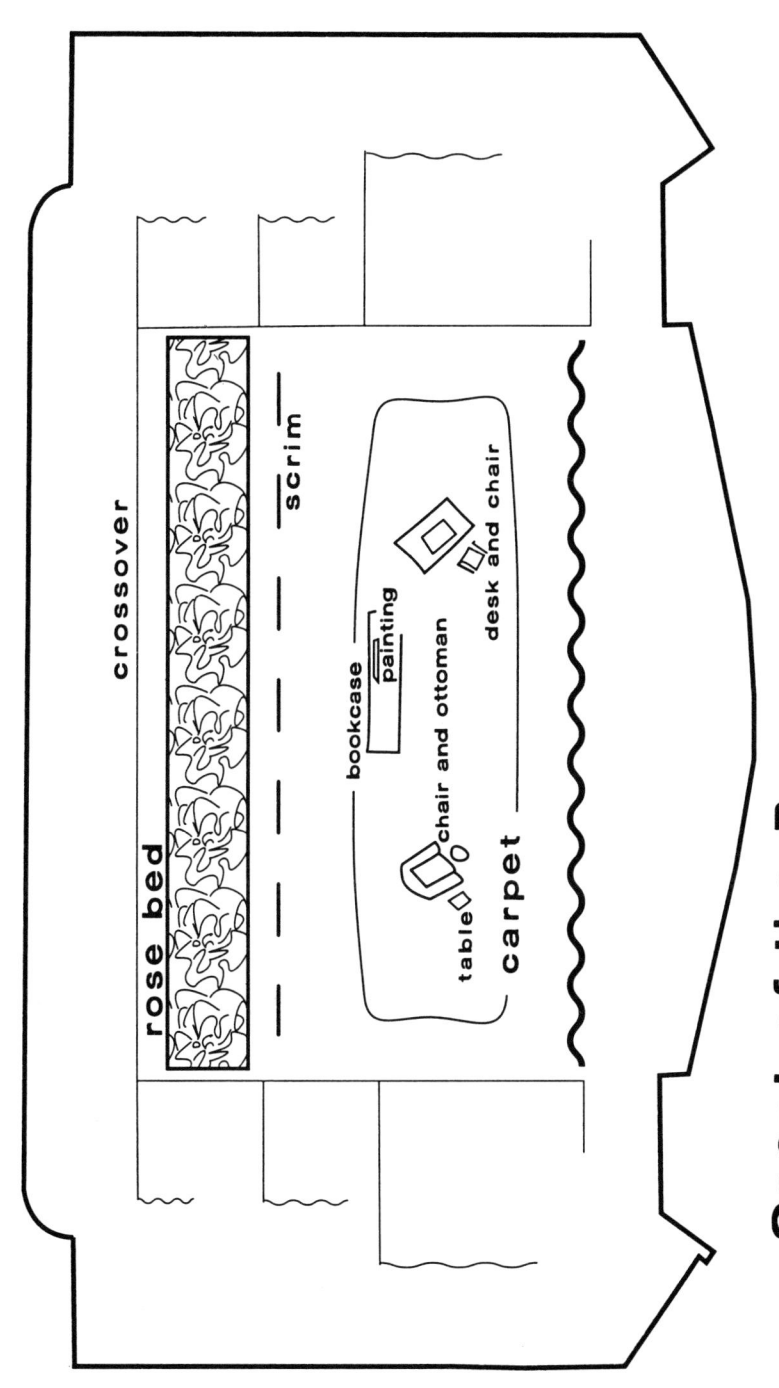

Scent of the Roses
set design by Thomas Lynch

NEW PLAYS

★ **HONOUR by Joanna Murray-Smith.** In a series of intense confrontations, a wife, husband, lover and daughter negotiate the forces of passion, history, responsibility and honour. "HONOUR makes for surprisingly interesting viewing. Tight, crackling dialogue (usually played out in punchy verbal duels) captures characters unable to deal with emotions ... Murray-Smith effectively places her characters in situations that strip away pretense." –*Variety* "... the play's virtues are strong: a distinctive theatrical voice, passionate concerns ... HONOUR might just capture a few honors of its own." –*Time Out Magazine* [1M, 3W] ISBN: 0-8222-1683-3

★ **MR. PETERS' CONNECTIONS by Arthur Miller.** Mr. Miller describes the protagonist as existing in a dream-like state when the mind is "freed to roam from real memories to conjectures, from trivialities to tragic insights, from terror of death to glorying in one's being alive." With this memory play, the Tony Award and Pulitzer Prize-winner reaffirms his stature as the world's foremost dramatist. "... a cross between Joycean stream-of-consciousness and Strindberg's dream plays, sweetened with a dose of William Saroyan's philosophical whimsy ... CONNECTIONS is most intriguing ..." –*The NY Times* [5M, 3W] ISBN: 0-8222-1687-6

★ **THE WAITING ROOM by Lisa Loomer.** Three women from different centuries meet in a doctor's waiting room in this dark comedy about the timeless quest for beauty – and its cost. "... THE WAITING ROOM ... is a bold, risky melange of conflicting elements that is ... terrifically moving ... There's no resisting the fierce emotional pull of the play." –*The NY Times* "... one of the high points of this year's Off-Broadway season ... THE WAITING ROOM is well worth a visit." –*Back Stage* [7M, 4W, flexible casting] ISBN: 0-8222-1594-2

★ **THE OLD SETTLER by John Henry Redwood.** A sweet-natured comedy about two church-going sisters in 1943 Harlem and the handsome young man who rents a room in their apartment. "For all of its decent sentiments, THE OLD SETTLER avoids sentimentality. It has the authenticity and lack of pretense of an Early American sampler." –*The NY Times* "We've had some fine plays Off-Broadway this season, and this is one of the best." –*The NY Post* [1M, 3W] ISBN: 0-8-222-1642-6

★ **LAST TRAIN TO NIBROC by Arlene Hutton.** In 1940 two young strangers share a seat on a train bound east only to find their paths will cross again. "All aboard. LAST TRAIN TO NIBROC is a sweetly told little chamber romance." –*Show Business* "... [a] gently charming little play, reminiscent of Thornton Wilder in its look at rustic Americans who are to be treasured for their simplicity and directness ..." –*Associated Press* "The old formula of boy wins girls, boy loses girl, boy wins girl still works ... [a] well-made play that perfectly captures a slice of small-town-life-gone-by." –*Back Stage* [1M, 1W] ISBN: 0-8222-1753-8

★ **OVER THE RIVER AND THROUGH THE WOODS by Joe DiPietro.** Nick sees both sets of his grandparents every Sunday for dinner. This is routine until he has to tell them that he's been offered a dream job in Seattle. The news doesn't sit so well. "A hilarious family comedy that is even funnier than his long running musical revue *I Love You, You're Perfect, Now Change*." –*Back Stage* "Loaded with laughs every step of the way." –*Star-Ledger* [3M, 3W] ISBN: 0-8222-1712-0

★ **SIDE MAN by Warren Leight.** 1999 Tony Award winner. This is the story of a broken family and the decline of jazz as popular entertainment. "... a tender, deeply personal memory play about the turmoil in the family of a jazz musician as his career crumbles at the dawn of the age of rock-and-roll ..." –*The NY Times* "[SIDE MAN] is an elegy for two things – a lost world and a lost love. When the two notes sound together in harmony, it is moving and graceful ..." –*The NY Daily News* "An atmospheric memory play ... with crisp dialogue and clearly drawn characters ... reflects the passing of an era with persuasive insight ... The joy and despair of the musicians is skillfully illustrated." –*Variety* [5M, 3W] ISBN: 0-8222-1721-X

DRAMATISTS PLAY SERVICE, INC.
440 Park Avenue South, New York, NY 10016 212-683-8960 Fax 212-213-1539
postmaster@dramatists.com   www.dramatists.com

NEW PLAYS

★ **CLOSER by Patrick Marber.** Winner of the 1998 Olivier Award for Best Play and the 1999 New York Drama Critics Circle Award for Best Foreign Play. Four lives intertwine over the course of four and a half years in this densely plotted, stinging look at modern love and betrayal. "CLOSER is a sad, savvy, often funny play that casts a steely, unblinking gaze at the world of relationships and lets you come to your own conclusions ... CLOSER does not merely hold your attention; it burrows into you." –*New York Magazine* "A powerful, darkly funny play about the cosmic collision between the sun of love and the comet of desire." –*Newsweek Magazine* [2M, 2W] ISBN: 0-8222-1722-8

★ **THE MOST FABULOUS STORY EVER TOLD by Paul Rudnick.** A stage manager, headset and prompt book at hand, brings the house lights to half, then dark, and cues the creation of the world. Throughout the play, she's in control of everything. In other words, she's either God, or she thinks she is. "Line by line, Mr. Rudnick may be the funniest writer for the stage in the United States today ... One-liners, epigrams, withering put-downs and flashing repartee: These are the candles that Mr. Rudnick lights instead of cursing the darkness ... a testament to the virtues of laughing ... and in laughter, there is something like the memory of Eden." –*The NY Times* "Funny it is ... consistently, rapaciously, deliriously ... easily the funniest play in town." –*Variety* [4M, 5W] ISBN: 0-8222-1720-1

★ **A DOLL'S HOUSE by Henrik Ibsen, adapted by Frank McGuinness.** Winner of the 1997 Tony Award for Best Revival. "New, raw, gut-twisting and gripping. Easily the hottest drama this season." –*USA Today* "Bold, brilliant and alive." –*The Wall Street Journal* "A thunderclap of an evening that takes your breath away." –*Time Magazine* [4M, 4W, 2 boys] ISBN: 0-8222-1636-1

★ **THE HERBAL BED by Peter Whelan.** The play is based on actual events which occurred in Stratford-upon-Avon in the summer of 1613, when William Shakespeare's elder daughter was publicly accused of having a sexual liaison with a married neighbor and family friend. "In his probing new play, THE HERBAL BED ... Peter Whelan muses about a sidelong event in the life of Shakespeare's family and creates a finely textured tapestry of love and lies in the early 17th-century Stratford." –*The NY Times* "It is a first rate drama with interesting moral issues of truth and expediency." –*The NY Post* [5M, 3W] ISBN: 0-8222-1675-2

★ **SNAKEBIT by David Marshall Grant.** A study of modern friendship when put to the test. "... a rather smart and absorbing evening of water-cooler theater, the intimate sort of Off-Broadway experience that has you picking apart the recognizable characters long after the curtain calls." –*The NY Times* "Off-Broadway keeps on presenting us with compelling reasons for going to the theater. The latest is SNAKEBIT, David Marshall Grant's smart new comic drama about being thirtysomething and losing one's way in life." –*The NY Daily News* [3M, 1W] ISBN: 0-8222-1724-4

★ **A QUESTION OF MERCY by David Rabe.** The Obie Award-winning playwright probes the sensitive and controversial issue of doctor-assisted suicide in the age of AIDS in this poignant drama. "There are many devastating ironies in Mr. Rabe's beautifully considered, piercingly clear-eyed work ..." –*The NY Times* "With unsettling candor and disturbing insight, the play arouses pity and understanding of a troubling subject ... Rabe's provocative tale is an affirmation of dignity that rings clear and true." –*Variety* [6M, 1W] ISBN: 0-8222-1643-4

★ **DIMLY PERCEIVED THREATS TO THE SYSTEM by Jon Klein.** Reality and fantasy overlap with hilarious results as this unforgettable family attempts to survive the nineties. "Here's a play whose point about fractured families goes to the heart, mind – and ears." –*The Washington Post* "... an end-of-the-millennium comedy about a family on the verge of a nervous breakdown ... Trenchant and hilarious ..." –*The Baltimore Sun* [2M, 4W] ISBN: 0-8222-1677-9

DRAMATISTS PLAY SERVICE, INC.
440 Park Avenue South, New York, NY 10016 212-683-8960 Fax 212-213-1539
postmaster@dramatists.com   www.dramatists.com

NEW PLAYS

★ **AS BEES IN HONEY DROWN by Douglas Carter Beane.** Winner of the John Gassner Playwriting Award. A hot young novelist finds the subject of his new screenplay in a New York socialite who leads him into the world of *Auntie Mame* and *Breakfast at Tiffany's*, before she takes him for a ride. "A delicious soufflé of a satire ... [an] extremely entertaining fable for an age that always chooses image over substance." –*The NY Times* "... A witty assessment of one of the most active and relentless industries in a consumer society ... the creation of 'hot' young things, which the media have learned to mass produce with efficiency and zeal." –*The NY Daily News* [3M, 3W, flexible casting] ISBN: 0-8222-1651-5

★ **STUPID KIDS by John C. Russell.** In rapid, highly stylized scenes, the story follows four high-school students as they make their way from first through eighth period and beyond, struggling with the fears, frustrations, and longings peculiar to youth. "In STUPID KIDS ... playwright John C. Russell gets the opera of adolescence to a T ... The stylized teenspeak of STUPID KIDS ... suggests that Mr. Russell may have hidden a tape recorder under a desk in study hall somewhere and then scoured the tapes for good quotations ... it is the kids' insular, ceaselessly churning world, a pre-adult world of Doritos and libidos, that the playwright seeks to lay bare." –*The NY Times* "STUPID KIDS [is] a sharp-edged ... whoosh of teen angst and conformity anguish. It is also very funny." –*NY Newsday* [2M, 2W] ISBN: 0-8222-1698-1

★ **COLLECTED STORIES by Donald Margulies.** From Obie Award-winner Donald Margulies comes a provocative analysis of a student-teacher relationship that turns sour when the protégé becomes a rival. "With his fine ear for detail, Margulies creates an authentic, insular world, and he gives equal weight to the opposing viewpoints of two formidable characters." –*The LA Times* "This is probably Margulies' best play to date ..." –*The NY Post* "... always fluid and lively, the play is thick with ideas, like a stock-pot of good stew." –*The Village Voice* [2W] ISBN: 0-8222-1640-X

★ **FREEDOMLAND by Amy Freed.** An overdue showdown between a son and his father sets off fireworks that illuminate the neurosis, rage and anxiety of one family – and of America at the turn of the millennium. "FREEDOMLAND's more obvious links are to *Buried Child* and *Bosoms and Neglect*. Freed, like Guare, is an inspired wordsmith with a gift for surreal touches in situations grounded in familiar and real territory." –*Curtain Up* [3M, 4W] ISBN: 0-8222-1719-8

★ **STOP KISS by Diana Son.** A poignant and funny play about the ways, both sudden and slow, that lives can change irrevocably. "There's so much that is vital and exciting about STOP KISS ... you want to embrace this young author and cheer her onto other works ... the writing on display here is funny and credible ... you also will be charmed by its heartfelt characters and up-to-the-minute humor." –*The NY Daily News* "... irresistibly exciting ... a sweet, sad, and enchantingly sincere play." –*The NY Times* [3M, 3W] ISBN: 0-8222-1731-7

★ **THREE DAYS OF RAIN by Richard Greenberg.** The sins of fathers and mothers make for a bittersweet elegy in this poignant and revealing drama. "... a work so perfectly judged it heralds the arrival of a major playwright ... Greenberg is extraordinary." –*The NY Daily News* "Greenberg's play is filled with graceful passages that are by turns melancholy, harrowing, and often, quite funny." –*Variety* [2M, 1W] ISBN: 0-8222-1676-0

★ **THE WEIR by Conor McPherson.** In a bar in rural Ireland, the local men swap spooky stories in an attempt to impress a young woman from Dublin who recently moved into a nearby "haunted" house. However, the tables are soon turned when she spins a yarn of her own. "You shed all sense of time at this beautiful and devious new play." –*The NY Times* "Sheer theatrical magic. I have rarely been so convinced that I have just seen a modern classic. Tremendous." –*The London Daily Telegraph* [4M, 1W] ISBN: 0-8222-1706-6

DRAMATISTS PLAY SERVICE, INC.
440 Park Avenue South, New York, NY 10016 212-683-8960 Fax 212-213-1539
postmaster@dramatists.com   www.dramatists.com